The HEART of a SHEPHERD

Merry Christmas

The HEART of a SHEPHERD

Barbara Thom

WINEPRESS WP PUBLISHING

Printed in the United States of America

Cover Art by Jean Whitney

Illustration (p. 9) from Bible Art Series. © 1984. Used by permission of Standard Publishing Company.

Packaged by WinePress Publishing, PO Box 1406, Mukilteo, WA 98275. The views expressed or implied in this work do not necessarily reflect those of WinePress Publishing. Ultimate design, content, and editorial accuracy of this work is the responsibility of the author(s).

ISBN 1-57921-148-8
Library of Congress Catalog Card Number: 98-61305

CONTENTS

INTRODUCTION

THEY WALK THE DESERTS with their sheep. The grass they seek is sparse—a tuft here and another fifteen feet away. They wear the same type of ankle-length robes and sandals their ancestors did 2,000 years ago when Jesus walked the land. Sometimes they stop and find refuge from the 100 degree temperatures in the shade of their donkey or camel. Other times, they sit in caves, perhaps the same ones where David hid from King Saul. But, for the most part, they just slowly walk along, day after day, beneath the merciless sun.

"They are called Bedouins. Don't feel sorry for them," our guide remarked over the loudspeaker. "They may look poor, but this is their chosen lifestyle."

"Why would anyone choose a lifestyle like that?" a voice from the back of the bus demands.

I know.

We are glad to be in our air-conditioned bus as we travel from the Dead Sea toward Jerusalem. My husband takes the camera from my hands. "I think you have enough pictures of sheep now."

How different it all looks than what I had expected. I had been proud to be a shepherd back home; yet here, I don't know if I would even mention it. These shepherds look so unimportant, so poor.

Thoughts cross my mind. Why had God chosen to use shepherds for such important tasks in the Bible? Jacob, the father of the twelve tribes of Israel, tended sheep. Joseph, the young son of Jacob and Rachel, tended his father's flocks. He was chosen to save a whole continent from starvation. Moses was walking with his sheep when he came across the burning bush in the desert and was called to deliver all Israel from captivity in Egypt. David, the youngest of twelve, was chosen to be king of Israel by God. He spent all his young years with his harp, singing songs about God to his sheep.

What set these men apart from others? Was it the time they spent alone communing with God? Was it perhaps their humble lifestyle that caught God's attention? Or was it their shepherd's heart? Did God, the Good Shepherd, share a special relationship with human shepherds? Is that why God chose shepherds to be the first to see baby Jesus in Bethlehem? How I wanted the bus to stop so I could talk to these shepherds. My life had changed so much since I had left the city life and now had my own flock of sheep. Did these Bedouins in Israel know God as I did? Did they sing to their sheep like David did?

Later on our tour, we went to see some of the Dead Sea Scrolls. On one ancient parchment was a writing from David, in his own handwriting. My eyes welled up with tears as I read the interpretation of his words. I was the smallest of my brothers, the youngest of the sons of my father. So he made me shepherd of his flock.

It was written by a young man who didn't know what God had in store for him. He had not yet met Goliath. He had no dreams of being a king. He was content. He was a shepherd.

I felt a kinship with David. I am the youngest in my family, and for some reason God chose to let me experience what it is like to have a shepherd's heart. As I tended my sheep, the Lord revealed to me the depth of His love for us, His sheep—an incredible, self-sacrificing love like none other.

© 1984. Used by permission.

CHAPTER 1

THE PROMISED LAND

MY GOOD SHEPHERD, JESUS, had a plan for my life just as He has for yours. In order for this plan to develop, He had to get me, a city girl, to move to the country. Once that was accomplished, He had to deal with my lifelong desire to have horses. I was forty, and my back was not as young as it used to be. The horses lasted only a little while.

My husband thought we should raise cattle, but we couldn't get the steer we bought at an auction into the back of our pickup truck. Instead, it broke loose, jumped over the cab of the truck, and ran through two fences and a cemetery before we were finally able to chase it back to the auction yard. We gladly left it there. Through trial and error, we finally found out what God's plan was. We were to be shepherds.

Sheep are not as productive living on acreage that is dried up. Without good pasture they will be thin and often have just one lamb a year. But move them to a pasture of clover and fresh grass, and they will have twins and sometimes triplets. God needed to move me to a different pasture so I too could be more productive. Sometimes God has to use a crowbar to get us to change lifestyles. This was the case with me. I liked city life. The thought of living in an area where there was mud instead of sidewalks was not very appealing to me. But as we all know, God can do anything. Eventually, He put His desire in my heart, and when at last I wanted to make the move, I could not. Something was blocking God from answering my prayers. I was about to learn a very important lesson.

As new Christians, we had already found out how real God is and seen incredible evidence of His love. God likes us to participate in prayer. He likes to see our faces when His actions and our prayers meet hand in hand to bring forth a miracle. He is overjoyed when He can bless us with an answer. "You have not because you ask not." Ask! Give God every opportunity to bring you a miracle. He delights in doing it. But prepare yourself. Not all requests turn out like you think they should. You may have some interesting side journeys to get where you think you are going.

We had lived in the city all of our lives. Then, when two of our three children started skipping school and dabbling with drugs, we decided moving to the country might be the answer. We had been living in a beautiful home in Bellevue, Washington, an upper-class neighborhood of mostly doctors and lawyers. Apparently many of the kids in the area were buying drugs with money stolen from their parents. Peer pressure was getting the upper hand. When counseling and grounding got no results, moving seemed to be the only answer.

We put our house on the market just as interest rates started their fast-moving climb to 22 percent. My job was selling real estate, and my husband was a plumber. Both jobs were connected to the housing market. Not only was it a hard time to sell our own home, but almost impossible to earn an income. The transactions on the twelve homes I had worked so hard to sell or list were falling apart, and all my projected income with them. Soon it was hard to make our payments, and the only choice left was to give the house back to the mortgage holder and leave.

My husband, Alan, and I started looking at farms to rent that were half the amount of the payments we had been making. All we found were rundown, filthy places I would not want a dog to live in. We were both sick with concern of what to do. Why were our prayers not answered? Why wasn't God helping us? We had put $30,000 down on that house and paid five years worth of high payments. We had already signed the papers to give them back the house, and we had two weeks left before we were out in the street.

Then something happened that taught me a great deal about unanswered prayer. I have to go back a few months to set up this most interesting and astounding beginning.

My husband worked with a contractor who invited us to his home to celebrate Jesus' birthday. This was our first Christmas as Christians, and we were thrilled to attend. I found the contractor's wife, Ginny, to be an extraordinary woman of God, who, in my eyes, glowed with anointing. She was kind, gracious, and prayed like an angel. Her hair was golden, her eyes were a soft blue, with sweetness and purity radiating from them. And wise! I couldn't believe the wisdom that poured forth through her every statement. I was sure she had every verse in the Bible memorized, and she was so willing to share her wonderful knowledge. On top of that she seemed to want to be my friend.

Ginny told me about a Christian women's meeting she attended once a month and invited me to go with her for lunch the next week.

That Thursday I found myself sitting with about 150 other ladies at the Red Lion Inn. We were having a wonderful time over lunch while listening to a very nice looking speaker. She was sharing a remarkable story that had happened several years back. To the best of my memory, she had been diagnosed with a terrible disease that among other horrible things, made her hair fall out. She had no friends except for a very old dog with arthritis, and she had lost her job. At this point in her story she felt there was no hope. There was no money and only a can of pop left in the refrigerator.

She was about to swallow some pills to kill herself when a knock came to her door. It was a pastor who had just opened a new church down the street and had stopped by to invite her to come. He noticed that she had been crying and invited himself in. After talking for a while, they found they had both come from the same town back east and had other common interests. She, not having a visitor or phone call for several months, had genuinely enjoyed the conversation. Upon leaving, he handed her some money and told her he believed the Lord was telling him that she was to paint a picture of Jesus for his new church. She confessed never to have painted or even drawn anything before in her life, but he insisted that God had told him she could.

The story ended with a woman who gave her life to Jesus, recovered from her terrible illness, and painted not just one famous picture of Jesus, but many. She was now a well-known artist and speaker.

I attended monthly and loved to hear the stories of God's wonderful love and mercy. Meanwhile, my new friend and I were really enjoying each other's company. Then information came out about a retreat. Ginny asked if I would like to go with her. It was three days long, and we would share a dorm with several other ladies I was getting to know and admire. This sounded so exciting. I said yes immediately and went home to share my joy with my husband.

Shortly thereafter I stood in a large conference room with about 500 women singing beautiful songs to the Lord. I closed my eyes and could actually picture us at Jesus' throne singing with angels. The music was so beautiful. I felt I was growing in leaps and bounds. I had been so blind the thirty-five years before I met Jesus to what went on in the spiritual world. I was totally filled with love and joy. I had never been so happy. I glanced over to Ginny. Tears were streaming down her face, but they did not look like tears of joy.

I put my arm around her, trying to comfort what I did not understand.

"What's wrong?" I quietly asked her.

She poured out a story of how she felt God had wanted her to start a program similar to this for teenage girls. She felt totally incapable of taking on such a large responsibility.

"No problem," I offered. "I will help you. We both have teenage daughters. Let's tackle it together. You be Moses, and I'll be Aaron. It will be fun."

I'm sure she did quite a bit of praying first, something I had not yet learned should be done, but within a month or two we had our first meeting for girls. It was really neat doing something so wonderful with my daughter, giving her a taste of what I had been so blessed with, but Ginny seemed to be really stressed out and not doing too well.

She decided which girls should be in leadership, and I offered my advice on why those were not good choices.

Being a successful realtor for many years, I felt quite capable at making good on-the-spot decisions. I had a very strong personality and felt quite confident in myself. After only a few months she asked me to just pray during the meeting and not offer any more help. I was insulted. Then, when that didn't work, she asked me not to come anymore. My daughter could, but I could not.

I was crushed. I cried for days. I had been fired from a volunteer job by someone whom I had totally trusted and loved. She didn't call me, and I didn't call her. I didn't understand why she had done this to me. When my daughter, Lisa, left to go to her meetings, I felt betrayed. Surely she would stick up for her mother, but off she went seeming not to care at all about what I was going through.

Then one day at church the subject of forgiveness came up. I knew God wanted me to forgive Ginny. So, through gritted teeth I said, "I forgive her, Jesus." The anger and rejection continued throughout the week, so I said it again. "I forgive her, Jesus."

Nothing seemed to change. I resented her more and more each time my daughter went to a meeting or visited with her daughter on the phone. Then one day while reading in Matthew, I ran across a verse that made my hair stand on end. "Forgive," God said, "or I will not forgive you."

Oh, I thought, *this is serious. I have to forgive her.* I tried and tried, and after some time passed I seemed to just forget about her. I had not been attending the Christian women's meetings for several months now, and I decided I would go to the next retreat. After all, why should I let her stop me from growing in the Lord and enjoying the meetings?

I arrived feeling very alone. I tried to make some new friends with my dorm mates and then went to the first meeting. There she was, up front with a prayer counselor badge hanging from her lapel.

How can she counsel people when she just about caused me to walk away from God? I thought to myself. Suddenly the truth hit me right between the eyes. I had not forgiven Ginny. My time there was miserable. I could not worship. I had no joy. I could not seem to forgive her. I had been hurt so deeply there seemed no way out. I went home very discouraged.

Time passed, and one morning at five-thirty my daughter Rebecca came into my room with the bad news her car wouldn't start. She needed a ride to work. It was a beautiful clear morning, crisp yet not cold, as we drove the short distance to the laundromat where she was employed. She had been complaining that her stomach felt upset, so I offered to go back to a little market after I dropped her off and get her a 7-Up. There was little traffic as I pulled into the large, carless parking lot. I chose to park a few aisles out just because the morning was so pretty and I wanted to walk a little. I bought the 7-Up and returned to my car, opened the door, and got in.

To my great surprise, a woman suddenly opened the passenger door and asked me if I was a Christian. She was a grandmotherly looking lady, around fifty-five I'd guess. So I was startled, but she didn't frighten me. "Yes," I answered "I am."

She reached across the seat to hand me a pamphlet and said, "God wants you to have this."

I glanced down at the pamphlet. The words were as incredible as the circumstance under which I had just received them: *How to Forgive*. It must have taken me a full three seconds to glance down and then back at her, but to my amazement she was no longer there. The car door was shut, and there was no sign of her anywhere. I got out of my car and ran around to the other side, thinking she must have fallen, but she was not there.

I went back into the store, asking the cashier if he had seen her. There was not even another car out there in the lot for her to be hidden by. She was gone. I may have given up on my forgiving Ginny, but God had not.

Many years later I did a study on angels and found that everyone I interviewed who had an angel experience said the same thing. They wait for you to look away for a second, and then they disappear. God had gone to great lengths to see that I was able to forgive.

I'd like to say that did it, I forgave and everything was rosy, but even that could not seem to get me past the rejection, anger, and hurt still in my heart. But God still did not give up on me.

I knew so little about the Bible, I had been concerned that people would put me down. Nearly a year had passed, and I had joined a small group of women in a Bible study at a dear lady's home. I still had so much to learn. The ladies were all older than I, but they made me feel very welcome and were patient with my many questions.

I remember reading about God being a jealous God. I was quite distressed that we had all been worshiping Jesus.

They showed me verses so I would understand that God the Father, God the Son, and God the Holy Spirit are all one, and put my mind to rest. I did not bring up my problem with unforgiveness, but their gentle prayers over me seemed to make me feel loved and peaceful anyway.

Then one day I got a call from Peg, the lady in whose home we met. She was planning a Passover feast and wanted to know if I would like to come. It would be at her home, and only eleven of us ladies were invited. I was so grateful to be one of the few.

When I arrived I looked in awe at a beautifully set table. As people began to sit down, I found there was nowhere left to sit except two places. One was at the head of the table and had been set with an elegant gold service and plate and a stunning red goblet. The other place setting was very nice too, but nothing near the elligence of the beautiful red and gold one. Even though red is very appealing to me I decided it would be best if I took the other seat next to it. When I found out that no one sat there, I questioned why. "That seat is for Jesus," I was told.

I was overwhelmed with the love of my precious Savior. It was if He had saved that seat especially for me right there next to Him. I had just been reading about how the mother of James and John, the disciples of the Lord, had been told, "You know not what you ask" (Matt. 20:22) when she had asked if her sons could sit next to Jesus on His throne in heaven. Yet there I was, sitting at His right hand. His love was so incredible to me that I was finally able to forgive. Tears of joy ran down my cheeks. I was back in my Savior's arms again.

That was two weeks before we had to move out of our foreclosing home to heaven only knew where. As I left Peg's home later that day, I noticed her next-door neighbor had an adorable little farm with shutters and window boxes filled with pretty red flowers on her chicken coop. "Please, Lord," I prayed, "can I *please* have a farm?"

At the corner stop sign I looked up into an extraordinary sight. There in the sky was a beautiful, vibrant, double rainbow. It was as if God said to me, "I promise."

As I arrived home, the phone was ringing. I threw open the door trying to catch it before they hung up.

"Is this Mrs. Barbara Thom?" a businesslike voice queried on the other end.

"Yes it is," I replied.

"This is Mary from Metro Mortgage. We have a check for you. Would you and Mr. Thom have time to come down and pick it up today or tomorrow?"

We had sold a house on contract eight years before, and the people had cashed us out. We picked up a check for $28,000 later that afternoon.

The dam in our river of prayer had been dislodged through forgiveness.

Within two weeks we had bought a twenty-three-foot trailer to live in and purchased a seventeen-acre tract of land in Snohomish, Washington. They wanted only $12,000 for the down payment and would carry the contract for the balance at an exceptionally low interest rate.

We named it the "Promised" Land, drew up plans, and started construction on our new three-thousand-square-foot home. We, like Joshua, saw no giants ahead.

We had faith that God would supply the rest of the funds, and He did. Not that it was easy. I told my husband after living without electricity and water for the first six months that I thought God had us in training to be missionaries! But slowly and steadily He provided all we needed.

I am convinced that so many prayers are blocked by unforgiveness. Clench your teeth if necessary, but take the first step. Nothing is more wonderful than being back in the flow of the blessings of our wonderful Lord and Savior. Remember, He has forgiven you.

CHAPTER 2

❧

PROMISED LAND SHEEP

GOD WENT BEYOND OUR greatest expectations when we asked Him for guidance in finding our new Promised Land. We had no idea the move would be such a significant one. The new adventure brought revelation we could not have experienced if we had remained in the city. We gradually experienced a new depth of understanding about His plan for our lives.

God told us to go north, and through Scripture He said, "the land would be divided." He also gave us a verse about the Jordan. Driving around with our realtor, we felt we were on the right track when we saw the Jordan Road. We headed around a lake and at one end saw a beautiful piece of property with two FOR SALE signs on it. It had been divided into two parcels.

We started work on our new home in September. Building it ourselves saved a lot of money. But living with a twenty-year-old son and a fifteen-year-old daughter for the first four months in a twenty-three-foot travel trailer with no electricity and no water was quite a challenge. Our older daughter, Rebecca, chose to get an apartment and stay in Bellevue, where her job was.

By Christmas time we had all the framework done. We were so anxious to move in and get out of the cramped quarters of our little trailer, we ventured the move in before the insulation had been put up. In Washington it's pretty cold at Christmas time, so we spent the first night huddled close to the wood stove.

Lisa had signed up for the FFA (Future Farmers of America) at school and needed a project animal. We wanted to get some chickens so we had built a small shed and chicken coop with our chainsaw while we had been waiting for permits to build our house. When Lisa announced there were two free lambs at school, we thought we had a real bargain.

Then the truth came out. They were not lambs, but very wild, pregnant sheep with minds of their own.

The agriculture teacher helped us get them home in his van. Upon arrival he said he would get the first sheep headed in the right direction. All my husband had to do was grab the neck of the other. She would then, supposedly, follow the one the teacher was leading to her new home. Ha! Ha! They immediately went in two different directions with two grown men in tow. No one was headed anywhere near the chicken coop. This farming was not as easy as it looked. These critters, though smaller than the steer, were pretty strong-willed too.

Finally settled in, we found sheep were not as dumb as people made them out to be. They discovered that chicken wire was easily bent, and they proceeded to crawl under it to freedom. They stayed near the house, however, and we discovered they could be lured back to their shed with a little grain in a coffee can.

We soon found out our new friends were totally defenseless and a favorite morsel of coyotes. I was awake nightly with worry. Our land is backed up to 500 acres of forest land. We not only had an abundance of coyotes, but also bear, deer, and an occasional cougar.

By the time our lambs were born, we had constructed what is called a New Zealand fence: seven strands of very potent hot wire. My husband tested it by accident and assured me nothing in its right mind would go through it. Sleep at last.

Soon our daughter was entered in the local fairs, and we were at work training these wild woolly critters to be show sheep.

We sheared them. A couple of months later, when they had about an inch of wool, we bathed them in Wool-Lite. What a job. Soap suds everywhere—more on us than on them. Then we put a lead rope on them and started training them to walk with us. Some lay down stubbornly; some jumped three feet in the air when the rope was tugged on. But after several hours they led readily, especially if you were headed toward the barn.

Then came the real challenge. We took off the lead rope and held them with one hand under their chin, put their feet in place with the other hand, and . . voila! Show sheep.

Mom and Dad got terribly attached to these fuzzy little creatures after a while, especially after Romeo and Julio, our first lambs, were born and the mother sheep rejected Romeo. So many lessons have to be learned the hard way, and sadly this was one of them.

A neighbor had been called because we felt our ewe was having difficulty giving birth to her first lamb. The little guy was saved, but because our neighbor's scent was now on him and was unfamiliar to our ewe, she decided that he was not her lamb. Nothing we could do could convince her otherwise. If he got anywhere near her, she put her head down and butted him mercilessly. So our first lamb melted our hearts and wound up a bottle baby.

Our destiny was cemented. We were to become shepherds—God's plan for us, I am sure, all along.

CHAPTER 3

WISDOM

I ALWAYS GET BENT OUT of shape when people call sheep dumb. They do dumb things sometimes, kind of like us. But they are teachable.

At first, lambs eat every two hours, so it was easiest to keep our new little lamb, Romeo, in a box in the house. After two weeks, he was old enough to run in the field with his brother, but he needed a bottle every four to five hours. Each time I went outside, he was at my heels. He was devoted to his human substitute mother and gladly stayed by my side as I did my gardening. When I went out in the field for a rest, Romeo would snuggle up to me and put his little head in my lap. We became best friends, and I grew more and more attached to our soft, fuzzy-faced lambs.

Daily, Romeo would follow me 1,000 feet down our driveway to the mailbox. I would put the junk mail in his mouth, and he would prance up the driveway with me, happy to be of service. We taught another to shake hands, and several knew their individual names.

Then, one afternoon I watched the dog obedience program at the local fair. I watched how the dogs followed their

25

master, stopped when he stopped, crawled through a large pipe on command, passed up a dish of dog food, brought their master their leash, then sat at his side. I was greatly inspired to enter my little friend. Romeo could do all that, and I was sure he would have no problem passing up the dog food.

I filled out an application form and called him a sheep dog. Sorry to say, they wouldn't let us participate when they saw my sheep dog. They said his scent would confuse the real dogs too much, but it sure would have been fun. Perhaps too, it would have helped to dislodge the belief that sheep are dumb.

God's sheep are no different. Without the patience and teaching of a Good Shepherd, we go blindly about our lives, making a lot of mistakes along the way. Before I gave my life to Jesus, I thought I knew it all. Being a late-in-life child, I had longed for a family of my own. I married young and had three darling children by the time I was twenty-three. I rocked them, sang to them, nursed them, adored them. I called them endearing little names. They were always clean and dressed well. They never sassed me. I had done everything "the correct way" and was just about to write a book on how to raise good kids. I considered myself moral, honest, and pretty smart, but I had a big surprise ahead of me.

I had watched the movie *The Ten Commandments* on TV when I was young and figured I would live by them. I expected my family would also. It was hard, but I thought I was doing pretty well. The thing that was missing, however, was a relationship with the Author of those commandments and the grace and forgiveness for error. We did not go to church, read the Bible, or even talk about God.

Everything seemed to be going along just fine. Then one night Rebecca, my thirteen-year-old daughter, didn't come home for dinner. At first I was angry. Her dinner sat there on the table getting cold. But when it got dark, and the other two kids were in bed, we started to get worried. There had been no warning signs that anything was wrong. The night was cold and unusually dark. I went up to her room. Her rainbow bedspread was covered with favorite stuffed animals. On her dresser lay her button collection. "One of a kind," "Hot Lips," "99% Angel" I picked up several remembering when and how she got each one. Nothing was out of place. Nothing to give me any idea of what was happening.

Rebecca was a beautiful girl barely 5' tall with deep blue eyes. Her long golden hair had a slight wave to it, and was always clean and shiny. She was a joy to be around, full of unexpected wit and charm.

I stood alone in her room looking out the window into the dark. "Where are you Becka where are you?"

We called the police at midnight, after exhausting all attempts at locating her by calling her friends. The wait was long and cold as we sat in our kitchen, listening to the clock tick all night long. Had she been killed or hit by a car? Why hadn't she called? We couldn't just sit there waiting any more, so we took turns driving up and down streets and calling hospitals. I had read stories in the paper about other parents with children missing and the terrible things that happened to them. I never dreamed I would be experiencing this horror.

The whole next day we heard nothing. I felt I would loose my mind with worry. My husband stayed home from work, but there was nothing we could do but sit by the phone and wait. Where was my baby – thoughts of kidnapping – rape – even murder played havock with my mind.

Two days later one of her girlfriend's mother found a piece of paper in her daughter's bedroom with air-flight information on it. Her daughter was missing too. It took three long days to locate the two of them. They had taken the money out of their bank accounts and bought tickets to San Francisco. Their plan was to work at night and sleep in the day on the beach. We were in a state of shock when we heard where they were.

They ran out of money; it was raining; and they had spent the three days sleeping in a phone booth in a hotel lobby. When the police escorted Rebecca from the plane, she could not look us in the eye. She would not talk to us.

I could not understand why she was acting like this. She had been well cared for all her life. We had taken our kids on all our vacations. Now that she was old enough to finally be able to communicate with us, she wouldn't. Friends suddenly had more influence than parents. We all went to counseling, but even with this, things seemed to be getting worse rapidly. She had put up a wall and none of us could get through to her.

Time passed, soon she had a boyfriend. I came home from work early one day and surprised them. She had not used any contraceptive. I didn't know where to turn or what to do. A friend at work suggested I take her to Planned Parenthood. There, they confirmed my fears and advised abortion. I told them I didn't believe in abortion. They told me it was not my decision. It was my fourteen-year-old daughter's life. She decided on the abortion.

I had to pay cash to a receptionist at the doctor's office. Rebecca didn't want me to come in with her, so I waited while the abortion was performed. She came walking out a couple hours later and shrugged my arm off her. "I'm able to walk on my own, Mom."

What had happened to my family? Having a loving happy family was all I had ever wanted. Why was everything such a mess? I was angry, hurt, confused, helpless.

We nursed Rebecca back to health over the next week. Then one night, after we had all gone to bed, we heard her boyfriend in her room again.

My husband threw him out by the scruff of the neck while I tried to contend with Rebecca. The whole family was either crying or mad or upset. There didn't seem to be any getting through to our daughter. Meanwhile, we discovered, Rebecca and our son, Mark, were getting more and more into the drug scene.

I called the counselor the next day, who advised me to throw Rebecca out. "She'll find out how rough life is out there and be back before you know it."

"You can come back when you can be a good girl," were my final comments to her.

How I wish it could have been that simple. She didn't come back. Days turned to weeks, weeks turned to months. I heard rumors of her running with a pack of boys. She was living in cars or at friends homes or in a boat with her boyfriend—whatever was handy. They robbed a house and were shot at by the owner, who had come down the stairs and caught them. When I arrived at the police station to pick her up, they told me she didn't want to see me.

"Then put her in detention," I said.

I turned my back and left. I was angry at her attitude. Perhaps that would put some sense into her. What had I done to deserve this?

The next day the local newspaper recounted the story: "Mother rejects 15-year-old daughter at police station." There went my integrity.

I tried to listen, but she wouldn't talk. I tried to be understanding, but I couldn't figure her out. I tried being strict. I tried being loving. I felt like I was in a car skidding on ice. I had my foot on the brake and my hands on the steering wheel, but I had no control. Nothing I did could stop the coming crash. I was so concerned with the dangers of her living on the streets, I finally surrendered to her strong will.

"Come home, Rebecca. Let's try to start over." I tried to reason with her.

"Not without Steve," she stubbornly replied.

Steve, her boyfriend, had been living on the streets with her, and she was not about to abandon him. There was nothing I could do. My morals were too high to allow two fifteen-year-olds to live together in my home.

Nothing worked. Then she more or less disappeared for a while. I didn't know where she was, and I was nearly to the point that I didn't care anymore.

I had been to the doctor on a regular basis, getting muscle relaxers and finally cortisone shots for the stress I was experiencing. I was still trying to deal with our son, and I would snap at my little girl for no reason at all. I cried nearly every day. Then the big blow came.

I had just gotten my family off to school when the phone rang. It was Steve's mother.

"Steve called me a few minutes ago and said Rebecca had tried to kill herself. She took a bottle of aspirin with a bottle of champagne. She has been throwing up blood for three days."

She told me where I could find her, and I was out the door. Soon, I stood knocking at her apartment door. A junior-high schooler answered.

"Is Rebecca here?" I asked in a near panic tone.

"That's for me to know and for you to find out" was his uncaring answer.

I pushed my way in, waded through sleeping bags, beer cans, and garbage bags full of fast-food wrappers. I found her lying in a bedroom on the floor. She was as white as a ghost.

"Come home with me, Rebecca."

I knelt beside her, brushing her long blonde hair back from her face. My heart was breaking seeing her like this.

"I'm not happy there, Mom."

"Well, you're not happy here, or you wouldn't be trying to kill yourself. Come home with me, and I will do everything in my power to make you happy," I promised.

She let me help her to her feet, and together we struggled out the door, down the stairs, and into my car. I laid her on the couch when we got home, and I called the doctor to find out where to take her. I started making her some soup while I awaited his return call. Then I heard a loud bang, bang, bang, on my front door. It was Steve.

"Did you barge into my apartment and take Rebecca?" he demanded.

"I can't believe you let her throw up blood for three days before you let anyone know," I angrily responded.

"Well, you never gave a ———! about her anyway!" he yelled back.

Suddenly Rebecca got up off the couch and left with him. My heart sank. What had I done? I had promised to make her happy, and the first thing I did was attack her boyfriend. She needed medical attention. I called out to her, but she just kept walking. I was desperate.

I called the suicide prevention hotline. "She has to call, not you."

I called her counselor. "She has a wall around her twelve feet thick. I can't seem to reach her."

I called her probation officer. "Nothing I can do. She hasn't broken parole."

My husband was my only hope. He was due home soon. I sat waiting for his arrival.

When I told him she had tried to kill herself and asked him to go and get her, his weary answer was, "What do you want me to do, tie her in a chair?"

There was nowhere else to turn. I hated him for letting me down. I went to my room, threw myself on my bed, and sobbed.

It was two days before Mother's Day. I had promised my niece I would go to her church to hear her sing. Church didn't mean anything to me. I figured it was just a social thing, a place where people went to look good. That Sunday, I made myself get up and get dressed and go to her church. My head was splitting. My shoulders ached. I was miserable. I sat next to my husband, among about four hundred strangers. I wasn't listening to the sermon. I was bent over, holding my aching head in my hands, thinking to myself, *I am so confused. I don't know what to do or where to turn.*

The pastor suddenly stopped the whole service. He said, "I'm sorry, but someone out there is crying out to God. You are so confused you don't know what to do or where to turn. God wants you to know you can turn to Him." My head came up as I listened to words that shot through my body.

He continued, "If you feel like you have the weight of the world on your shoulders, give those burdens to Jesus. He died to set you free. If it is your child that you are worried about," he pointed up in the air, "He is her Father. You can trust Him." I could hardly believe the words I was hearing. God was real! And He could hear me! And He cared.

"Would you stand so we can pray for you?" the pastor asked.

I was shaking all over. I pushed myself to my feet as several wonderful people gathered around me. They put their hands on my shoulders and on my head. I felt the burdens coming off. I felt the pain leaving my body as they prayed. I gave my daughter to Jesus with great relief that there was Someone I could trust with my precious baby.

When I got home from church that day, Rebecca was standing in my kitchen. She gave me the first hug she had given me in nearly three years.

Pride comes before the fall. I thought I knew it all. I thought I could have a happy marriage and raise the best kids around. But I knew nothing. God started showing me what unconditional love is. He showed me how I had broken the commandment, "Thou shalt not kill," when I had hatred in my heart. I had not loved God and had plenty of gods before Him. A controlling spirit was at the root of my marriage and parenting. My anger, I found out, was a form of self-centeredness and would arise when I lost that control. I had been full of pride and self-confidence, but I soon found out just how little I could do without God.

Slowly, Sunday after Sunday, as we attended church, God counseled us through the messages that seemed to be just for us. We began reading our Bible and repented daily as He showed us our sins. God changed our hearts. The change in us was so dramatic that our daughter wanted it too. We took our eyes off the problems and put them on Jesus. We had a home filled with joy and peace for the first time ever. It was a miracle. Only God could have put our family back together.

Wisdom, I have found, comes from surrender to our Shepherd, Jesus. It comes through obedience to God, Who is real and wants nothing but the best for us. We grew by allowing Him to teach us. We learned a lot by reading His Word and going to church. Living by the law, being good, just doesn't do it. God wants to help us. With His wisdom, guidance, and a teachable spirit, God's sheep can learn to be wise too.

CHAPTER 4

❧

HE CALLS US BY NAME

AFTER A COUPLE YEARS of working with crossbred sheep, we decided we wanted to get some purebreds. Adults cannot show crossbred sheep in competition, but they can show purebreds in what is called an *open class*. So we bought our first two expensive sheep.

Soon they lambed, and we had an adorable little boy and girl we named Pride and Joy. After all, they were our pride and joy. Joy was doing very well and bounced happily around the barn. But Pride stood hunched in a corner, his eyes dull, his little ears drooping. I watched them nurse, thinking maybe the mother was rejecting this little one. But that was not the case. The only thing I could gather is that his attention span seemed to be very short. He would not nurse continually, like the little girl lamb, until his tummy was full.

We tried a bottle supplement, which he refused. We tried staying with him when he nursed to keep him there and interested, but nothing seemed to work. He was gaining about a pound a week compared to her six pounds. His frame was growing bigger, but his flesh didn't fill out. We knew we were growing dangerously close to losing him.

Then one day I was reading my Bible and a thought struck me. God doesn't like pride. Pride is a sin. It separates us from God. Was God trying to tell us something? We prayed about it, anointed him with oil, and renamed him Elisha's Bones. After all, a man came back to life in the Bible when his body touched Elisha's bones. Immediately he began to gain weight. His tail began to wag, and he bounced around the barn a little smaller but determined to make up for lost time.

We knew in the Bible names were important. They meant something. God was teaching us something through what we named our sheep. "He calls his own sheep by name and leads them out. When he has brought out all his own, he goes on ahead of them, and his sheep follow him because they know his voice" (John 10:3).

We named one Moses only to realize that when he died, Moses did not enter the Promised Land. We named one Rachel only to discover that Rachel was barren until God finally opened her womb. We named one Lazarus and sold him to a little girl to show in a contest. Several months later we went to see her show him. He was smaller than his projected weight because he had nearly died after being attacked by a coyote. He went through massive surgery and then nearly died again after developing an infection. But somehow he had made a miraculous recovery and won the competition out of 163 sheep! We became a lot more cautious about what we named our lambs after that.

Some know their names as I call to them. Years later Joy still responds to us when she's standing in the middle of a flock of sheep and we call her name. Her head pops up, her ears alert, and she maneuvers her way through the crowd until she comes happily to stand before us for her pat on the head.

Satan, on the other hand, thinks of us as another notch on his gun. He is not interested in our name, just how he can deceive us into becoming his sheep. Over the years, we have seen many sheep owned by people who neglect them. They are mangy, underfed, and live in terrible conditions. Those sheep are ear tagged with a number, never having been called a name or knowing the personal care of a good shepherd. They are just one of a number of sheep. Part of a flock, they are just a means to earn money for their shepherds.

We made a big sign that read "Promised Land Sheep" and little cards above all their pens with their names on them at the fairs. "Peace, Patience, Joy, Prophet, Samson." We had a message to tell those who came by: "Jesus Loves Ewe."

One year one of our sheep gave birth to triplets. We named the third little girl Blessing because we saw her as an extra special gift from God. She was very little, perhaps only four pounds at birth compared to her brother and sister who were a good ten to twelve pounds. Needless to say, she got pushed out of the way at dinner time, so, not wanting to lose her, we started feeding her a bottle. She became quite friendly because of all the extra attention she was getting, but by no means would she ever make much of a show sheep.

Then one day a lady called me. "Do you have any little friendly lambs for sale? I'd like to get a pet for my children, but we don't have very much money."

"Well, yes, I have one," I replied hesitantly, hating to part with her, yet knowing I had to.

They were out within the hour. The woman got out of the van and then helped her nearly blind son out. She opened the sliding side door as wide as possible so another child, about twelve, could watch from her wheelchair. Another little girl about six hopped out on her own.

We walked into the barn, where my husband and I had corralled the smaller lambs to be ear tagged. They "ooo-ed" and "ah-ed," and the boy reached down to pet one.

"Which one is ours?" the little girl asked excitedly.

"Yours is around the back with the older lambs. These are too young to be able to go home with anyone yet."

A touch of disappointment was audible in her "Oh." But as we turned the corner and I called Blessing, delight reentered her voice.

Blessing was no bigger than the ones inside, even though she was older. For some strange reason beyond me, she ran straight to the children, who quickly swept her off her feet and into their arms. "Is this her?" the wide-eyed children asked.

"Yes, that's her," I replied happily, knowing this lamb was going to a good home.

The mother turned to me and asked, "Her name is Blessing? Are you people Christians? Our daddy just went to jail for seven years, and we really needed a blessing at our house."

It is interesting to see the details God is concerned with in our lives. To even help us name a lamb because He knew those people needed a blessing. Our names are important to Him too. He writes them in a book in heaven as the angels rejoice when we find our Savior.

CHAPTER 5

HOPE

BECAUSE WE ENJOYED our sheep and spent so much time with them, they were extremely gentle and tame. We let kids at the fairs get in the pens with them. One little boy happened by one day and asked if he could pet our sheep. When we opened the pen and let him in, you could see the delight in his eyes, but then a sadness came as he looked up at me and said, "I wish I could have a lamb."

He was nine years old, his daddy had abandoned the family, and his mother and sister and he had to move into a small trailer with their grandpa. There was no land or any place to play in the trailer park, and he longed for a better life.

"Well," I tenderly put my arm around him, "do you know how I got my farm? I prayed and asked Jesus for it."

"Do you think He would answer my prayer?" the little blue eyes gazed up at me, hoping to believe.

He received not just hope that day, but a wonderful Savior, Who, unlike his earthly father, will never leave him or forsake him. Jesus is a God of hope. He loves to bless us.

God found a way of reaching the lost through our little hobby. He gave us the delight of our hearts, and we were the delight of His. God is so good. "Trust in the Lord and do good: dwell in the land and enjoy safe pasture. Delight yourself in the Lord and he will give you the desires of your heart" (Ps. 37:3–4).

Children are easy to reach for Jesus yet many who go to Sunday School are never asked if they want to give their hearts to Jesus. There are many dangers ahead of them in life. They need to know more than Bible verses. They need to know God is real and that He hears their every prayer.

CHAPTER 6

॰॰

LET YOUR LIGHT SHINE

WE WERE AT THE OREGON STATE FAIR just after the Gulf War began. Our Promised Land sign over the sheep pens drew larger crowds than usual. We were learning a lesson about letting our light shine. Little did we know to what extent people recognized the light we displayed until this particular week.

It seemed everyone who stopped by wanted to know if we thought the Gulf War was the beginning of the war of Armageddon.

We were overwhelmed with visitors from all walks of life, and we were able to meet many of their fears with assurance that they too could know the way, the truth, and the life. When we let our light shine, God is sure to bring someone by to see it.

Many people are homeschooling their children and for good reason. As we seek God in prayer, however, we realize some can go into the public schools and be a light to the lost. Jesus did not stay with the saved, but mingled with the

41

sinners. Seeking God's guidance on this is very important. Looking through the Bible, I found this passage:

> Sons are a heritage from the Lord, children a reward from him. Like arrows in the hands of a warrior are sons born in one's youth. Blessed is the man whose quiver is full of them. They will not be put to shame when they contend with their enemies in the gate. (Ps. 127:3–5)

Children are hard to defeat when they're brought up in the ways of the Lord, filled with the Word of truth, are aimed by praying warriors (parents), and then sent forth into their schools. They bring light into dark places and set captives free wherever they are. They are bold, Spirit-filled "J" bombs set to light up the sky with God's power and knock the socks off all Satan's plans.

After we had seen our first two children fall into bad company in junior high school, we made the hard decision to leave our youngest in the public school system anyway. We felt assurance from God this was the right decision. Lisa, unlike her siblings, had found the Lord at a young age and was a committed Christian. She was very active in church plays and was solid in the Lord very early. She had watched her brother and sister cause a lot of heartache and problems, and I think she had learned a lot from their mistakes.

Lisa brought friends and their parents from her school to see her in the plays the church put on, and many were saved. When she got older, she participated in school talent shows and sang Jesus songs. Later she was asked to sing "Friends," by Michael W. Smith, for their school annual, which was done that year in video form.

When she got involved with the Future Farmers of America, she won the opportunity to go back to Kansas City, Missouri, with 23,000 other young people to compete in one of many fields for best in the nation. She had won the Washington State talent field and was blessed to sing before all of them right before they left to come home. She sang "People Need the Lord."

Later that night one of the planes carrying eight of our kids and four leaders from Idaho went down in Colorado, killing them all. The Lord had given Lisa the opportunity to reach out to them that night. I know He tries even to the last second of our lives to reach us. I pray the words to that song were in their minds those last few minutes and they gave their lives to Jesus.

I had one of those last-chance experiences with a woman while visiting my mother-in-law, who was in the hospital with a stroke. My sister-in-law had mentioned a very thin old lady in the next bed who had refused to eat for several days. No one had come in to visit her. She had given up and was lying there wanting to die. While the nurses were busy with Mom, I walked over to the old woman's bedside.

"Do you know about Jesus?" I asked her quietly.

Her sad brown eyes glanced up at me as she shook her head no.

Beginning with Genesis, I gave her an overview of God's plan. She gave me a not-so-nice look, abruptly rolled over in her bed, and turned her back on me. She apparently didn't want to know.

But something in me kept going. I told her how God was with us right there in that room and how He would never leave her or forsake her. He had given his only Son for her, and even if her mother and father had forsaken her, God would not. I stayed about an hour. She motioned for me to leave occasionally in the beginning, but when I did not give up, she finally surrendered to listening.

Who knows how many people had tried to reach her? Who knows what kind of a life she had led to wind up all alone with no one by her side in her final hours? Yet God did not give up. He sent me.

When at last I came to the end of my message to her, I walked around the bed. I noticed a tear drop dangling from the bridge of her nose. I held out my hand. "Would you like to ask Jesus to forgive your sins and come to live in your heart?" I gently asked her.

"Yes," was the only word I ever heard her say as she put her hand in mine. But, oh, what a beautiful word. She gave her life to Jesus that night. When I called in the morning, she was gone. Gone to be with Jesus. Safe in His arms of love.

God tries to the very last minute. We have such a wonderful gift to give if only we will let that light shine. We do not know now if any of the people Lisa sang to received Jesus before the airplane went down, but we know Jesus made every attempt at reaching them. It is a miracle she was able to sing about Jesus in a public school setting to begin with. God knew what they needed to hear that night, and Lisa was obedient to deliver it.

Later, when it became harder and harder to mention Jesus in school, Lisa was going to junior college. She was soon to attend commencement exercises. There would be no pastor to pray over the graduating students that year because of the accelerated separation of church and state. They were looking for someone who could sing a couple of appropriate songs for the evening and heard that Lisa sang. They made the mistake of not asking her what she would sing.

The keynote speaker was a well-known columnist who was obviously into New Age thinking. She mentioned the wisdom of the Dali Lama. She suggested those stuck in old traditional thinking patterns were like frogs in a pot of boiling water. She spoke of the insight our children could achieve by watching the Ninja Turtles on TV. My heart sank as I watched that woman get a standing ovation from all those naive people who didn't recognize the Pied Piper was leading them away from their Good Shepherd.

Nervously Lisa walked over to the piano and gave the music to the accompanist. She had chosen "Pray for Me, and I'll Pray for You." It couldn't have been more appropriate. God used our little girl all the way. We are glad Lisa was a light who could make such a wonderful difference in such a darkening world.

No matter what you are doing, no matter where you are, there are people all around you who need to hear about Jesus. He is the most wonderful gift we can give anyone. If we get a box of chocolates, we may be unwilling to pass around our box, because there will be none left for us. But each time we share Jesus, there is more of Him to go around. Go into the world, and let your light shine.

CHAPTER 7

~~

HIS YOKE IS EASY

MATTHEW 11:28–30 SAYS, "Come to me, all you who are weary and burdened, and I will give you rest. Take my yoke upon you and learn from me, for I am gentle and humble in heart, and you will find rest for your souls. For my yoke is easy and my burden is light."

If His yoke is easy, why do we struggle so much over the decisions we face? Perhaps we need to strengthen our trust muscle.

Now that we were official shepherds, it was time to buy our first ram. We excitedly packed our bags and were off to Oregon to check out what the breeders down there had. After several visits to many of the larger breeders, we found him. He was about five months old, and his rate of gain so far showed us that he was going to be *big*. Just what we needed. The judges at the fairs seemed to like them that way.

We named him Sir Lancelot. (This was before we started using Bible names.) We also bought a ewe we named Guinevere from another farm and happily headed home.

Lancie, as we started calling him, was extremely affectionate. He greeted us as we came up the driveway by running alongside our car, jumping with all four feet off the ground at once. He seemed almost to dance his way up to the gate for his scratch under the chin. We learned you do not pat rams on the head. They think you want to play war games if you do, and they always win. He loved attention, and soon we had him sitting perched on his back legs and raising one foot to "shake hands." This was really cute until he weighed over 450 pounds and was six or seven feet high when standing on his back legs.

He won lots of awards for us, and everyone marveled at his size. His lambs were wonderful too, until one was born with serious defects. Examining X-rays of the lamb, we discovered that our beloved ram had a defective gene. If he mated with a ewe with similar gene problems, she would have nothing but deformed lambs. We also learned that this was not just our problem. Many people had purchased lambs sired from this bloodline because they were so much larger than other sheep, and they were all facing the same problem.

Our hearts hit bottom. We could not sell him, knowing we might pass on this gene to another farm. We could not keep him. If we got another ram, they would probably try to kill each other. Because of his size, he would probably win. The only other choice was to put him and his offspring down.

Tears poured down my cheeks as I anguished over this decision. He was a joy to us all. How could this awful thing happen to us? I could not bring myself to make the decision, yet each day that went by, the hurt grew worse. I woke in the middle of the night, got up, and looked at him from my bedroom window. He lay there peacefully in the moonlight. He was so strong, so healthy looking.

I tossed, I turned, I prayed. My depression grew worse and worse. I cried through every song they sang at church about a lamb.

Six weeks went by. Every day I was tormented by the thought of putting him to sleep. Then, one night as I was going to bed I said to God, "I can't do this, Lord. If he is not supposed to be here, then take him. Do something. I can't."

In the morning we found him a few feet from his shelter, lying on his side, dead. We could find no other apparent reason for his death other than God had taken the burden off my shoulders. Perhaps Satan had wanted to destroy our small flock. Perhaps he wanted us to be tempted by pride for having the biggest sheep around. Whatever the case, when I turned my hopeless state over to God, the stumbling block was removed.

Although it hurt to lose him, we knew it was the best for us all. (I tell all my sheep about Jesus and hope to have quite a flock in heaven someday. After all, the Bible says to preach the gospel to all creation, doesn't it?)

We prayed again and asked God to weed out this gene from our flock. We sold all the little boys (ram lambs) as market lambs and kept the little girls (ewe lambs). The vet told us that each little girl had a 50 percent chance of being a carrier. After that, each of their lambs had a less and less percentage of being a carrier. Within seven years the chances would be near zero, as long as we bred them to rams with clean bloodlines.

Out of those three that we kept, over approximately ten years, the line has produced only eight female lambs. We kept none of the ram lambs but sent them to market, even though we never had another deformed lamb born. Some ewes miscarried; some newborn lambs were stepped on or smothered by their mothers. Compared with other bloodlines, the losses were much higher. While it still hurts to lose those lambs, quite often at birth, I know God is in control. He can see and do what we cannot.

When hard decisions have to be made, God does not want us to suffer over them, but to trust Him. It mentions in the Bible that the disciples often chose lots or drew straws to make choices, praying of course that God would direct them.

We can see an example of this in the opening chapter of Acts. The disciples were trying to decide on a replacement for Judas. Notice that first they used their knowledge and best judgment to select men who had been among them at the time Jesus was with them. Second, they prayed and put the matter in God's hands. Third, they drew straws and trusted God was making the decision for them. The passage reads:

> Therefore it is necessary to choose one of the men who have been with us the whole time the Lord Jesus went in and out among us, beginning from John's baptism to the time when Jesus was taken up from us. For one of these must become a witness with us of his resurrection.
> So they proposed two men: Joseph called Barsabbas (also known as Justus), and Matthias. Then they prayed, "Lord, you know everyone's heart. Show us which of these two you have chosen to take over this apostolic ministry, which Judas left to go where he belongs." Then they cast lots, and the lot fell to Matthias; so he was added to the eleven apostles (Acts 1:21–26).

My husband's niece, Jeryl, a petite girl about five feet tall, married a man over six feet tall with a large frame. When it came time to have children, the first had to be taken caesarean, weighing nearly nine pounds.

When Jeryl became pregnant again, she wanted to try to have a normal birth. After many hours of labor, the doctor confronted them with a problem. "This is a bigger baby than what we had anticipated. We need to do another caesarean or use forceps. The delivery with forceps can be dangerous to the baby. What do you want to do?"

Our niece was in no shape at this point to make a good decision, and there was no time to do any research. Her husband prayed for the Lord's guidance, and then pulled a coin out of his pocket. "Heads, it is born natural," he said. He flipped the coin into the air, trusting that God would tell them what to do. The baby was born natural—a healthy ten-pound, six-ounce boy they named Daniel.

God wants to help take burdens off our shoulders. He wants to guide us and help us make our decisions in life. There are many ways He can communicate with us. While flipping a coin is probably the last means we would choose to hear from Him, God will use any means we give Him to be able to communicate with us in desperate times. Truly His yoke is easy when we realize God is on our side. When we learn to trust Him with all things, we will find He wants nothing but the best for us.

CHAPTER 8

EMMANUEL

LIFE ON OUR SMALL FARM, the Promised Land, was challenging but enjoyable. I loved raising sheep. Over the years it has become clear to me why God compares sheep with His children. In many ways I too viewed my sheep as more than animals but as very special members of my family.

One fall we decided to enter some of our sheep in a competition at a fair in Yakima, Washington, about a five-hour drive away. Since we would be gone for five days, we asked my daughter's friend, Linda, to feed our sheep. She would be responsible for six ewes, each of whom had twin lambs.

When we chose names for the last set, a ewe lamb and a ram lamb, we decided on Emily for the little girl. I had grown attached to the name Emily as the result of listening to a song on the radio in those days. We named her and then began trying to think of a name that also started with an *e* for her brother.

He was a chunk of a lamb, definitely all boy. His feet were too big for his body, and his face was nothing but a little black nose and two sparkling brown eyes that peeked out from a fuzzy mass of downlike wool. He was a little clumsy because he was growing faster than his coordination could keep up with. He was a lamb you couldn't help but love. The name Emmanuel came to mind and seemed to fit. He was special. But then I had second thoughts. After all, that was God's name. But then again, it meant "God is with us," and He is. So that became our little guy's name.

We loaded up the sheep that were going to the fair, and I gave last-minute instructions to our little helper from next door.

"The sheep are fed twice a day. A flake of alfalfa and one-half can of grain each," I told her. The lambs had their own little area to eat in called a *lamb creep*. It looked like a large playpen with spaces nine to eleven inches wide. Only the lambs could get through, which kept their mothers from eating their food.

"The twelve lambs get a bucket full of a special mixture of grain with just a little sprinkle of corn, oats, and barley to flavor it up," I told her. "It's kind of like candy to them so don't give them too much. You feed them twice a day, and they also get three flakes of alfalfa."

We had put lots of nice, fresh wood shavings down for them and had piled straw in the corners of the barn for the lambs to snuggle up in at night. I showed her where everything was stored, and she seemed to understand just fine. We thanked her for her willingness to help and returned to packing.

It was a cold October morning when we left. Dark clouds filled the sky, and rain was in the forecast. Over the mountains, the weather would be dry and sunny. We were anxious to be on our way, and yet we had never left the sheep for any length of time before. Something in me wanted to stay. Perhaps it was my shepherd's heart.

The five days were busy and fun, but the fair rules required that we couldn't leave the grounds until the fair closed at 11:00 P.M. We could have spent one more night there, but we were anxious to get home. After a hard day of showing sheep, we packed gear and equipment and set out on our long drive home.

We arrived in the pouring rain at 5:30 A.M., weary from sitting so long and just plain exhausted. We let our show sheep out of our horse trailer into a nearby pasture with a shelter, then I headed to the barn to check on our babies. The mothers were all in there with two little lambs each nestled against their warm, woolly bodies as I glanced around the barn. There was Devotion with her two lambs, Dedication and Compassion. There was Eden with her two lambs, Elisha and Elijah. When I looked at Emmanuel's mother, however, she had only one lamb by her side. Emmanuel was missing!

I looked behind her in all the nooks and crannies but couldn't see him anywhere. I had never seen a mother ewe leave a lamb before. If one was stuck somewhere, usually the mother kept bleating until I noticed and went to help. But this mother sat there contentedly chewing her cud as though nothing was wrong.

I called out to my daughter to check the upper pasture. My husband headed for the house, looking for a note from the neighbor saying Emmanuel was at the vet or something, and I headed for the lower pasture. It was still dark. The rain was coming down in torrents. Our flashlights were not much help, and we could not hear any response to our calling.

Soon, my husband returned from the house. No note had been found. We walked and walked until we were drenched, looking under bushes, fearing a coyote had somehow gotten in. Still there was no sign of our little lamb. My husband gave up and went in. My daughter came back empty handed. We were both shivering from the cold, so I told her to go in too. I was bewildered. There was no sign of him anywhere. With nowhere else to turn, I turned to

God. "Please, Lord," I prayed, "if he is alive, please help me to find him. I don't want to leave him out there in the cold."

No sooner had the prayer left my mind than I heard a weak little "baa" coming from the adjoining pasture, just forty feet from where I was standing. He was lying on his side, able to move only his eyes. Soaking wet, he was heavier than I could carry, so I ran to the house to get help from my husband. Emmanuel's body seemed stiff and nearly lifeless as Alan gathered him in his arms and brought him into the house by the fire. We called the vet, who told us to massage him to get his circulation going, try to give him liquids, get him warmed up as much as possible, and then bring him in at 7:30. He could not swallow, so we did the best we could with everything else and wrapped him in a big blanket to get him to the vet.

Upon arriving, we were told to lay him on a cold steel table in the middle of the room. The vet looked in Emmanuel's eyes, listened to his heart and stomach, opened his mouth and looked in, and then stood back from the table.

He told us that our lamb had been grain poisoned by eating a large amount of corn oats and barley (the candy that was only to be sprinkled on top of the other grain) at one feeding. It had fermented in his stomach and turned to alcohol. It was the same as if someone had swallowed a fifth of whisky straight down. It had shut down all of his organs, and there was little or no hope for him at all. He recommended putting him down. When the vet was done speaking, the lamb looked from his face to mine. The little eyes, once sparkling and joyful, now reflected a worried look. It was as if he was pleading with me to help him. I was his shepherd, his only hope. Whatever I said meant life or death to him.

"We've got to try." God had caused him to cry out to me for help, I reasoned. He had kept him alive that long in the pouring rain. Surely He would not want it to end like this. My heart nearly broke when the vet said he had probably been lying there for two to three days to be in that condition and for his mother to leave him. Guilt took hold of my thoughts. If I had stayed home, this would not have happened to him. Poor little guy, even his own mother had given up on him.

The vet readied a pen for him in the dog kennel, where he laid him on his tummy with his four legs spread to keep his head in an upright position. He hooked up an intravenous feeding device and was going to just leave him there.

"Is it all right if I sit in there for a while?" I asked. "He may be frightened because of the dogs."

My daughter and I settled ourselves on the floor, and I rested his little head in my lap. "It's going to be all right." I tried to comfort him.

One of the assistants came in with a label to put on his door. It said "lamb." I had noticed the dogs all had their names on their doors, so I told her he had a name too.

"Emmanuel."

She seemed surprised by his name and went to make the change. On coming back she asked, "Is he a pet?"

"No, not exactly. We have twenty more at home."

"Is he a special show sheep or something?"

"Well, no, not really." He didn't have the qualities to be good enough for the show ring. He was just our lamb, and we loved him.

He eventually fell asleep. We laid his head back on the towel the vet had provided for him and slipped out to finally get a little sleep ourselves. It had been a long hard day in the life of a shepherd.

That evening we stopped in to see how he was doing. Not much of a change, although he recognized us when we came in. We again spent some time in prayer for him and rubbed his legs and back to try to get the circulation going again. We changed the wet towel under him. At least something seemed to be working. I was sure all the people at the clinic thought we were crazy to spend so much time with a lamb, but they were nice and let us in and out of the kennel area again.

The next morning, much to our delight, he raised his head when we came in. We were so excited, you could hear us all over the clinic. We enthusiastically thanked God and began massaging our precious lamb with renewed confidence that he was going to make it after all.

We went home and decided the next visit that evening we would call his name like we do when we fed him at home and see if that would inspire him to try to get up.

The plan had grave results. His head popped up, but then suddenly he went into a convulsion. His little body got rigid, his eyes rolled back in his head. I told my daughter to get the vet quick. I held him in my arms, hoping he would relax. But another convulsion came and then another.

Questions hit my mind. *Am I making him suffer? Should I have let the vet put him down? Will he continue to have convulsions if he lives?*

I was upset and near tears when the vet came in.

"What do you want to do?" he asked. There it was again. I had to make the choice. The precious lamb I held in my arms depended totally on me. Then words hit my mind from out of nowhere. "The Lord giveth, and the Lord taketh away."

"OK, God," I responded audibly, wiping my tear-stained cheek, "You do it. He's in Your hands. I can't do it anymore, I can't stand to see him suffer." I decided to give him one more day.

The vet gave him a sedative, and he fell back to sleep. We left not knowing what the morning would bring.

I opened my Bible that night to read about God's sheep. John 10:11 says,

> I am the good shepherd. The good shepherd lays down his life for the sheep. The hired hand is not the shepherd who owns the sheep. So when he sees the wolf

coming, he abandons the sheep and runs away. Then the wolf attacks the flock and scatters it. The man runs away because he is a hired hand and cares nothing for the sheep. I am the good shepherd, I know my sheep and my sheep know me. Just as the Father knows me and I know the father and I lay down my life for the sheep.

Linda, our young helper, hadn't realized how severe the consequences would be when she treated the sheep to a whole can of the "candy" grain. She, with her busy schedule of school, homework, and caring for her own animals, had not taken time to make sure all the lambs were accounted for. They were not her lambs. She was the hired hand. I was their shepherd.

Even though I had been dead tired, the welfare of my sheep was more important to me than my own rest. I knew immediately which lamb was missing. God was showing me His heart for us. I read, "Though my father and mother forsake me, the Lord will receive me" (Ps. 27:10). Emmanuel's mother and his shepherd had not been there for him, but God was. God knows when a sparrow drops to the earth. He was there watching over my lamb until I got home. He gave that lamb the energy to cry out and then directed me to his side. The vet could not believe he could make a sound in his serious condition.

Even though I was at the point of giving up because I am but a human shepherd, the Lord never gives up on us. He is the Good Shepherd. If that lamb had not cried out to me, I may not have found him that night. In our desperate state, lost in the darkness of sin, God is looking for us, searching for His lost sheep. When we cry out to Him, He is there in an instant.

Some people have grown up neglected, abandoned, or reared by a "hired hand," never realizing the personal care of their true Shepherd. If this lamb had been you or me, the Lord may have found us drunk out of our minds in a gutter, but does He care what we have done? No, we are His sheep.

I didn't care if my lamb was a glutton or full of alcohol. All I cared about was his well-being. Nothing entered my mind about the cause of his desperate state; only my love for him and his dependence upon me mattered. He called out to me for help, and I was there. I hurt for him. I held him. I wanted nothing more than to see him restored to health and happiness.

The next day we entered the clinic to a buzz of joy. They were eager to give us the good news. On the third day Emmanuel, just like Jesus, rose again. Standing like Bambi on ice—legs spread wide but holding—we beheld our precious lamb. Never to have another convulsion, and forever to be a blessing to our lives, we took Emmanuel home to the Promised Land.

CHAPTER 9

❧

ONE SHEPHERD

IT IS ALWAYS FUN to have a new person come out to our farm to see our sheep. I love to watch their faces as I call, "Come on, pretty girls!" in a high-pitched voice. We stand at the gate and wait. Soon, off in the distance we see one, then two, then forty sheep coming from the upper pasture, kicking up their heels. They have heard my voice, and they leap in the air with excitement, knowing I am calling them.

Several people have tried to imitate my call, and some come quite close, but they cannot fool my sheep for long. They may get their attention momentarily, but a suspicion is in their walk.

They hesitate, then they stop at a distance and survey the situation. My husband, who helps with them daily, can call but nothing happens. They know my voice. They know one shepherd—me.

Many other religions outside of Christianity contain many gods, all who must be worshiped or appeased by sacrifice. Our God states that He is a jealous God. There are no other gods but Him.

My husband and I once went on a trip to Guatemala to see the Mayan ruins. Those ruins were incredible. There in the midst of a magnificent jungle stood stone structures nearly 200 feet high. We had a very knowledgeable guide of Mayan decent who told us not to stand on the large solitary stones in the front of several of those giant structures.

He went on to say his people were still offering sacrifices on those stones to this day. The park would be shut down so they could perform their religious ceremonies.

"What do they sacrifice?" I asked, not so sure I wanted to hear the answer.

"Chickens, mostly." He told us that the Mayans were a remarkable people who lived in the area dating back approximately 5,000 years.

They studied and worshiped the sun, the sky, and the stars, and came up with a calendar that is only seventeen seconds off to this day. They were also farmers and athletes. Their principal crop, corn, was their main source of food. When their crops began failing, they thought it must be an unhappy corn god.

Each year a great assembly of people gathered around a massive courtyard to watch a ballgame. Each village of people from all over the area brought their best ball player to compete in the games. The champion had the privilege of climbing the stairs of the pyramid where the high priest stood. There, he willingly died by heart extraction. His body was then allowed to drop down the narrow stairs of the structure, hopefully to hit the bottom, where his blood spilled out on the ground to appease the corn god. If it did not fall all the way down, the crops would surely fail. I could not help but notice how close they had come to the one true sacrifice. Jesus had to be the best too, and it is His blood that sets us free.

One big problem was that they did not know about crop rotation. The sacrifices increased. The chief and the chief's wife tried bloodletting from their own bodies. Her tongue was split, and his penis, but no matter what they did their crops continued to fail. They could not find a way to appease this god.

There were other gods as well who required sacrifice: the sun god, the moon god, the rain god. Carvings and pictures drawn on rocks are barbaric. Yet, this intelligent people could not find a way out of that vicious cycle.

Back on the bus, our guide then pointed out what he seemed to believe was a very special tree. The *ceba*—or as we know it the *kapok* tree—reaches high above the jungle. It is a host tree, and many ferns and flowers abide in its branches when it is not in bloom; otherwise, it would look barren. "This tree," he stated, "is the tree of life."

We were fascinated as he described how, in their mythology, the first man was made of dirt, but when the rain came he became mud, so they decided to make him of sticks. When he could not walk or talk, they finally decided to make him of corn. We were amazed at how close they were to biblical truth, yet through the grapevine, mythology had twisted and deceived them.

Then came woman. She went out into the ball court because a tree had grown there and was ruining the ball game. She took down and bit into a piece of its fruit, but it spit on her and she became pregnant. She gave birth to twins. One an artisan, the other a monkey. *The Darwin influence had even struck here,* I thought to myself.

He told us that through the tree of life, his people had found there were nine layers of the underworld and thirteen layers of the upper world. The top layer was heaven. His deep brown eyes looked sadly off into the distance as he remarked, "My people have never found their way out of the underworld."

My husband and I were sitting in the front seat of the tour bus, facing our small, interesting guide. "I know the way out," I told him.

"You do?" I had his full attention.

"Yes," I continued, "Jesus was the final sacrifice."

It was like a light came on inside him. He grasped it. We shared more on the topic from a Christian perspective and then asked him if he would like to accept Jesus as his Lord and Savior. He looked me straight in the eyes, confessed his sins, and asked Jesus into his heart right there on the tour bus in front of everybody.

"How do you feel now?" I asked.

"I feel really good," he said, "really good!"

Many cultures around the world serve many gods, but our God is a wise God. He knows too many gods, like cooks, spoil the soup. Too many dads in one family confuse the children, and too many religions erode the truth. God commands His people: "You shall have no other gods before me" (Exod. 20:3). He also said, "Hear O Israel: The Lord our God, the Lord is one" (Deut. 6:4). Finally Psalm 100:3 says, "Know that the Lord is God. It is he who made us, and we are his, we are his people, the sheep of his pasture."

You may ask, "If God is one, who is Jesus?"

Hebrews 1:4 reads: "So he became as much superior to the angels as the name he has inherited is superior to theirs. For to which of the angels did God ever say, 'You are my Son'?"

Jesus' name is inherited. If it is inherited, then it is God's name.

God also says, "But about the Son he says, 'Your throne, O God, will last for ever and ever'" (Heb. 1:8). God the Father labels God the Son as "God." He tells us to worship Him and to pray in the name of the Father, the Son, and the Holy Spirit because the three of them are one.

There is more to you than meets the eye as well. There is a spirit you, a soul you, and the you that is body. Yet, you are one.

Isaiah 9:6 tells us about Jesus 700 years before His birth. "For to us a child is born, to us a son is given, and the government will be on his shoulders. And he will be called

Wonderful Counselor, Mighty God, Everlasting Father, Prince of Peace." Isaiah has called the Son not only God, but also Father.

The Hindu people have embraced many gods. They worship the rat and watch their people starve as rats eat up nearly a quarter of their grain supply.

They worship the cow and let them wander through the streets, spreading disease into their water supplies as their people sicken.

Americans are welcoming similar Eastern religion as New Age—A religion that boasts we are all gods and goes on to say there is no truth. No thanks! I'm perfectly happy with the God who created me, who loves me, and in whom I have hope. He is one God in whom I am fearfully and wonderfully made. I believe in Jesus, who says He is the way, the truth, and the life. Christianity is the only religion that follows a God who loves us, who has experienced pain for us, and who brings us hope and joy. He is my Shepherd. Is He yours?

CHAPTER 10

⚮

TOO MANY SHEEP?

LAMBS ARE ADORABLE. You just want to gather them up in your arms and hug them. They grow fast and soon are mothers themselves. They can be bred very young, but we always waited until they were about a year and a half so they could gain full growth. Needless to say, we were keeping more than we were selling. After all, who could sell a pet who ate out of your hand and followed you everywhere? But things were piling up on me, and soon I was feeling overwhelmed with all I had heaped upon myself.

The pain I had in my shoulders was almost unbearable. For five months I had seen doctors, chiropractors, and therapists. Nothing seemed to help. Pain pills were no better than M&Ms, and muscle relaxants just made me tired. God was the only answer. I had been praying and had asked for prayer at our church. I was desperate when I went to our spring retreat. "Please, God, if You do nothing else, please just take the pain" was my only request.

The answer came near the end of the second day. *"I'll heal you one more time, if you'll let Me change your lifestyle."*

"Do it!" was my immediate response.

"*Read Ecclesiastes,*" was the next thought that came to my mind.

I had always thought of that book in the Bible as a real down and outer. This guy was really bummed out on life. But as I began to read, I started to see my problem.

"'Meaningless! Meaningless!' says the Teacher. 'Utterly meaningless! Everything is meaningless.' What does man gain from all his labor at which he toils under the sun?" (Eccl. 1:2–3). Then I read something that hit home. "I undertook great projects: I built houses for myself and planted vineyards" (Eccl. 2:4).

My husband and I had three houses that were nearly paid for in the Seattle area that we rented out. Since it was a fifty-mile roundtrip to take care of them, we had recently sold them and put the money down on two homes nearby and two apartment buildings. We could see that eventually we would be able to raise the rents on eighteen units instead of just three. We viewed it as an opportunity to build a better retirement savings. We hadn't really thought about all the extra work it would be. It didn't take long to find out that people don't stay in apartments nearly as long as they do when they move into a house. We did all the cleaning, painting, advertising, and renting the units out. What used to be a once-a-year event now was at least twice per month.

Ecclesiastes 2:5 says, "I made gardens and parks and planted all kinds of fruit trees in them." We were living on seventeen acres. I had planted twelve fruit trees twice. Both times, much to my frustration, my husband had mowed them with our tractor, thinking they were little alders.

My attempts at gardening were a failure. The weeds, no matter what I did, were three feet taller than anything I had planted. Boy, could I relate to that Solomon character!

Then came the biggie, midway through verse 7: "I also owned more herds and flocks than anyone in Jerusalem before me." Ouch! I had enjoyed my little flock so much that I couldn't sell them. I had nearly one hundred, and sheep require a lot of attention.

During the winter months, which in our area stretch from early October to June, they need to be fed twice per day. That means approximately five heavy bales of alfalfa and two bags of grain a day. They have to be wormed individually and given shots every two to three months. Their hooves also need to be trimmed (which is a really fun project). There are four hundred hoofs on one hundred sheep, and they don't like to stand still while you do it.

My husband held the halter and tried pinning them against a wall in the barn while I bent over and picked up one hoof at a time to trim. One sheep could take up to fifteen back-breaking minutes to trim.

Then comes lambing time. I had a really intense desire to be a good shepherd, and my heart broke if I lost a lamb. So I was up and out to the barn every two hours round the clock during lambing season, which lasts from December to February and sometimes into March. When I was exhausted, my husband and daughter pitched in. But if an ewe was giving birth, they would have to call me out anyway. Even with all my good intentions, sometimes a ewe would die, or she would get mastitis in her udder and require intensive care for up to six weeks. Unable to nurse from her, her lambs had to be bottle fed every two hours as well. I began to see what God was trying to tell me about stress.

On top of all this, I was now president of a women's ministry that required two to three nights of meetings and various duties to put our monthly meeting together. I was taking care of my two granddaughters, ages two and four, every Sunday and Monday while my daughter worked. I then had to spend Tuesday trying to put the house back together after their visit.

I cooked, cleaned, mowed, and helped get ten cords of wood in for winter, which was our only source of heat. My husband and I spent time discussing how best to invest in the stock market with the only money we had to fall back on. I was late everywhere I went and rushed from one thing to another, feeling guilty and insufficient in everything I did. I was tired, and I was *stressed*.

I had chest pains that turned out to be a spasming esophagus. I had shingles two years earlier, and my heart had been affected so I could no longer drink anything with caffeine in it. I had knots in my back and my jaws. I did not know how to relax.

Then I read Ecclesiastes 3:12: "I know that there is nothing better for men than to be happy and do good while they live." Is that all! *Wow*, I thought, *I can do that*. It was so easy. The thing that brought me the most happiness was sharing Jesus. I could do good and be happy all at the same time. The burden lifted. The weight came off. The pain vanished.

I brought home a new life. We hired a manager for our apartments and sold eighty sheep. I decided to let my husband make all the decisions about the stock market. The burdens were coming off. I told my daughter I would like to take care of my grandchildren once in a while, and my garden now consists of two rows of raspberries and two fruit trees that have a fence around them.

But God did not stop there. He also changed my attitude. My husband, being the easygoing type, could never keep up with my fast pace. I woke up, got dressed, made the fire, fixed breakfast, and fed the sheep by the time my husband took a shower and got dressed. Then he'd have to change clothes because he had put on clothes he didn't want to get soiled. By the time he got out to the barn to help me feed the sheep, I was done. It frustrated me daily.

Now, I work out on my treadmill or read while he takes his shower. Then I make breakfast while he gets dressed. We go out together to feed the sheep. And I'm happier than I have ever been, and I'm sure he is too.

CHAPTER 11

LET GO AND LET GOD

IS IT POSSIBLE TO BE TOO good of a shepherd? When it totally consumes you, the answer is yes. Sheep are capable of a lot more than I gave them credit for. So are people.

When we serve the Lord, we give Him free license to dabble with our temperaments. Not only did I discover my addiction to stress, but I was also to learn I had another problem with my "near perfect" personality.

When I accepted the position to become president of the Everett chapter of the women's ministry I enjoyed, my whole goal was to get those ladies out of the pews and working for Jesus. I knew Jesus taught His disciples for only three years and then said, "Go." Yet I saw so many people sitting in pews year after year, being fed and fed and fed, yet never getting up and going out to help others.

I thought I could change things. I would be the leader of the sheep, and they would follow, right? I knew, of course, it would take time. Wanting to follow God's instructions, I began praying.

The first year the Lord told me, "Build the wall."

When I asked Him how, He said, "Start with the foundation." So we got to know each other. We shared testimonies and formed our committees.

The second year, I asked the Lord, "What now?"

"Build the wall" was again His instruction.

"How, Lord?" I again inquired.

"With a sword at your side," came the reply. So that year, we did spiritual warfare for our community.

We got a vision of staking the land with survey stakes. The Lord told us to put a verse on one side to defeat the enemy of that area, and the other side to speak a blessing over it. He showed us in the vision that as the stake went into the ground, it would go through the head of a serpent that was the enemy of that area. I read much later about Jael putting a tent peg through the temple of Sisera, killing the enemy of Israel (see Judges 4:17–23).

Then God gave us Ezekiel 37:16–17, which says, "Take a stick of wood and write on it, 'Belonging to Judah and the Israelites associated with him.' Then take another stick of wood, and write on it, 'Ephraim's stick, belonging to Joseph and all the house of Israel associated with him.' Join them together into one stick so that they will become one in your hand."

The rest of the passage, through verse 24, said that God would join together the land and bring back His people. They would no longer backslide, but would live together, cleansed and free from idol worship, under one God. So we spent that year claiming the land for Jesus and speaking life into a city where the businesses were boarded up at the time.

I went to the mayor's office and visited with one of his staff members while waiting to see him. She was a Christian who was familiar with our ministry.

"Have you seen the angels arriving in Everett?" she asked me. Several people had been witnessing this most awesome event. They started coming about the same time we started claiming the land for Jesus. Three years later you could not find a business site available to rent anywhere. The whole city was bustling.

The third year, I asked God again, "What would You like us to do this year, Lord?" Again came the familiar words, "Build the wall individually."

We had arrived, I thought.

The Lord gave us a wonderful opportunity to do a fundraiser for the street kids in our area. We found out through a lady who was working with them that the main place that had been providing them meals for years was shutting down and that there were no Christian shelters for them anywhere in the city.

It was February when she took me to meet some of the kids. They were a strange-looking group on the outside, but as I watched guardedly, my opinion started to get holes in it. A girl ran back into the cafeteria. She was dressed in camouflage, army-looking clothes, complete with combat boots, a shaved head with a swastika tattooed on her neck, and black lipstick. I noticed she had forgotten her teddy bear on the table where she had been eating. She tucked him under her coat near her heart and walked out of the room. That's when my love for these strange-looking kids started to develop.

Another girl carried a rat under her thin coat. She had no shoes and nowhere to sleep, but the rat did. He had love and shelter. Another boy asked me if some pills he had would help him with congestion in his lungs. When I read the bottle and realized it was for pain, I asked him what he got them for.

"For frostbite." Suddenly, I could tolerate it no more. I went home and prayed, "What can I do?" and God answered. He called us to do a fundraiser for the kids. (I have discovered that when we see a need and pray "What can I do?" rather than "Oh, God, please help them," God will gladly put us to work. Those prayers turn into wonderful testimonies.)

We planned a play at an auditorium that seated 1,500 people. The actors were the street kids. Sheila, the lady who originally told me about the kids, opened her doors for our rehearsals. She had a simple one-bedroom apartment, but we got them all in. Another lady, Sandee, prepared a huge home-cooked meal for us all. We rehearsed, read the Bible, and prayed for their needs twice a week. We went through a lot of kids. They were transient. Just when I thought I had my cast, our Jesus character was thrown in jail for thirty days on a past warrant.

Several of them were sleeping under the freeway, got busted one night, and all wound up in jail.

But little by little we gained on it, several of the kids getting saved along the way. We could see God opening the eyes of the kids as they related to the play that was about a five-year-old girl whose parents divorced. Satan saw an opportunity to gain control in her life. He came up behind her and gave her toys to make her feel better—toys such as the nail of anger to get even with her parents for hurting her, or the rod of blame when she had no friends because of the nail of jealousy she used.

As she grew she used the toy of illicit sex to make her feel loved. But when the boy she had given her heart to left her wounded and depressed, she was brokenhearted. Finally, she was so desperate she turned to Jesus, who showed her the nails she had been using were those that nailed Him to the cross. He gave her a new heart as Satan slinked off stage and out of her life. The play is called *Broken Heart* by Linda Medill Hall. Our performance was a tremendous success, mistakes and all. About fifteen or twenty of the thirtysome kids we worked with asked Jesus into their hearts.

We took them all home to our farm after the play for a cast party. On the way I asked one who had been a gang leader if he had ever worked a regular job.

"You mean besides selling drugs and killing people?"

"Yeah," I replied, trying not to show any shock.

"Nah, there's no money in it," our nineteen-year-old friend confessed.

The play had made an impact on him, and as he attended a church that worked with kids like him, he made a decision to follow Jesus. He is now a roofer who goes to church twice a week and is bringing many more to the Lord as well.

I felt we had wonderful success. I felt great accomplishment in our being able to work together with several chapters of our women's ministry and churches as well. I had learned a lot about how to orchestrate a large event too. Six months later I thought we'd do another outreach.

We had some Christian friends who performed mime. They agreed to help us do a community outreach on Halloween. I worked very hard on advertising and even went door to door, personally inviting people to come. I made up fifty flyers and gave them to several of our girls to display in restaurants and stores ahead of time. As I made the rounds of the neighborhood, I realized no one had followed through on her job. The night of the performance only one hundred twenty people came. Most of them were from the church that lent us the chairs. Only six ladies from our women's group participated, and four of them were on my board. On top of that, only five people got saved. The offering that came in was less than if I had had a normal women's meeting with forty to fifty ladies in attendance.

I was let down, big time. Hadn't I led the way? Hadn't I done most of the work? Where was the support? Where were the people who were supposed to bring their unsaved friends? Where was God? Wasn't it His will to get people saved, that people serve, that we make enough money to do another one? Then why didn't God do His part?

I became depressed and couldn't seem to pull myself out. I felt I was in the desert. God quit talking to me or I quit hearing.

People gave me verses, such as, "Do not despise small beginnings," and, "God rejoices in finding one lost lamb," but nothing seemed to get through to me. I was mostly disappointed in the help. I had spent three long years trying to get these gals out of their pews to serve God.

Then, one day I picked up a book by Max Lucado entitled *He Still Moves Stones*. I read a story about Mary and Martha and saw that I had a Martha attitude! I couldn't believe it. I had known about Mary and Martha forever; but I never realized my zest to get others out of the pews, nonetheless to make God move, was a Martha attitude I had harbored in my motives. I confessed it as sin and asked God for His forgiveness.

The next day was my regular ministry meeting. Two young women came up after the meeting and asked me if I knew about impartation. Thinking it was some kind of new musical group, I said no. They explained that it meant passing your mantle on to another, like Elijah did to Elisha. "Oh," I said, "yes, I know what that is."

"We were wondering if you would pass your mantle of evangelism on to us."

"Take upon you my yoke, for it is easy." God had answered my prayer. All the effort I had put in to get women out of the pews failed. The Lord did it when I laid down my Martha attitude. "Let go and let God," as my prayer chairman kept preaching to me, became real. I understood.

God is not done with me yet. The hidden things appear now and then, and I grow more and more to understand my loving Savior's heart. He wants me to be free and happy and following in His steps. I do too.

Getting things done isn't as important to me anymore either. I try to do something that makes me happy everyday. I never used to have time to read much. Now I do. I said out loud every day, "I can't do it all," and I was right. I ran as fast as I could, and I couldn't get it all done. I used to be so tired, all I could do by the end of the day was plop in a chair in front of the TV. Now, I'm writing a book. Ecclesiastes 11:10 says, "So then, banish anxiety from your heart and cast off the troubles of your body." My body had suffered enough. God had set me free.

> He reached down from on high and took hold of me; he drew me out of deep waters. He rescued me from my powerful enemy, from my foes, who were too strong for me. They confronted me in the day of my disaster, but the Lord was my support. (2 Sam. 22:17–19)

Suddenly I saw the enemy, and he was me! I had brought all this upon myself.

But the next verse foreshadowed a happy ending: "He brought me out into a spacious place; he rescued me because he delighted in me" (v. 20).

> As for God, his way is perfect; the word of the Lord is flawless. He is a shield for all who take refuge in him. For who is God besides the Lord? And who is the Rock except our God. It is God who arms me with strength and makes my way perfect. He makes my feet like the feet of a deer; he enables me to stand on the heights. (2 Sam. 22:31–35)

God reminded me of a trip my husband and I had taken a few years earlier to Glacier National Park. We had seen a group of about twenty-five mountain goats and their kids climbing the jagged cliffs above us. When they got way up, they walked onto a glacier and slid, tumbled, and joyfully skidded all the way to the bottom. Then they climbed the rocks to do it all over again and again.

"Did you delight in watching them?" God spoke to my mind.

"Oh, yes, Lord. They were wonderful."

"That is how I want to delight in you, My daughter. I came to set the captives free, and who is set free is free indeed. Free from worry. Free from stress. Free from the need to control. Free to enjoy all I have created for you."

CHAPTER 12

NATIONAL CHAMPIONS

IN RENO, NEVADA, EACH YEAR a show and sale is held of some pretty nice-looking sheep. The first year we went, we were astonished at the prices people were willing to pay for a lamb. Five hundred to two thousand dollars was not uncommon. We watched as a one-year-old ram was sold for nine thousand dollars! I soon had my husband convinced that we could get those kinds of prices for our lambs too, if we bought some of these bloodlines.

The next year we went down with money in hand. We studied each ram the day before the sale, watched the show, and found one we wanted. He was just what we wanted, big and very classy looking. He had come from Wisconsin and took third place in his class. We prayed as the bidding got higher and higher. We had chosen not to go over one thousand dollars.

"Going once, going twice, sold." I threw my arms around my husband's neck. Boy, were we going to impress the competition back home.

I seemed to thrive on competition. I liked to win. Even as a child, I remember being proud of my perfect attendance record in school. I had held first position with my violin in orchestra all through junior-high school. At age nineteen, I took a job as a realtor and often won the award for top sales-person.

I had always considered myself confident, knowledge-able, able to make good decisions, and wanting nothing but the best for everyone. I was soon to find out that working with others was a little more difficult.

When I became president of my ministry chapter, I had a full board of five ladies, all volunteers like myself. I had made it clear to them all that we were serving God and we would be doing the very best job possible. I expected the fliers to go out before the first of the month. I expected the books to be balanced. I wanted every committee filled; and I expected all of them to be at every prayer meeting, picnic, and board meeting, with ideas, verses, and a word from God as to what direction we were to go the next month. Within a couple of months several were talking mutiny.

I went to my adviser, a very sweet older woman named Pat, not understanding why they would not want to do the best job possible. I could not comprehend why some did not come to scheduled meetings—some did not do their jobs at all—yet they still wanted to be on the board. I didn't understand why the attendees, knowing that I was an evan-gelist, would not bring the unsaved to the meetings. Things were not going well at all. I was doing my job and theirs too.

Pat looked at me with fright. "Oh," she said, knowing something had been wrong with our little group but not knowing what to put her finger on. "You may lose the whole board with those kinds of expectations. They are too high for anyone to reach."

We were at a conference, and the pastor, for some strange reason, was speaking on the same subject of high expectations. He told a story of how he and his wife came home late one evening after having ministered all day. His wife was so tired that she had decided to leave the dinner dishes and turn in early. He thought to himself, *She's worked so hard today. I'll do the dishes for her.*

But the Lord broke into his thoughts and said, *"Don't do them for her, do them for Me."* When Pastor Gary questioned God about that, God replied, *"If you do them for Me, you know I will appreciate your act of kindness. If she doesn't notice when she gets up in the morning, you will still be blessed. But if she does notice, you will be doubly blessed."*

By doing your work for God, as Pastor Gary did, it doesn't matter who notices. You have insulated yourself against the expectation of praise from another. You know God is pleased with you.

Discussing this further with Pat, I began reflecting back on my own expectations. My daughter Lisa had a beautiful voice. When she sang, people were moved to tears. She would be the next Amy Grant, and I would do everything in my power to see that she got there. My son was so handsome and intelligent, I couldn't understand why he refused to go to college. He was always interested in puzzles. He could be a famous research scientist if he would just apply himself. I expected my sheep to be national champions, and I even had a goal for myself to be the next Billy Graham.

Then I realized with regret how my high expectations could look like control and manipulation. I was hurting people with my perfectionism. I thought I was supposed to do the very best job I could, and so was everyone else, but really I was setting people up for failure. There was no way anyone could meet my goals for them. Not even me.

I started seeing it in other people, people who were placing goals and ideals ahead of people's feelings. It also revealed another ugly side effect. A critical, angry spirit evolves when someone doesn't meet our expectations, and tears into the other person's self-image. They were either slow or unwilling or incompetent but never good enough.

One man we knew cleaned the whole house trying to please his wife, but when she got home all she could see was the dirty washcloth in the sink he had been using. She focused on it and verbally tore him to shreds.

Another home was always in turmoil because the husband came home and immediately walked through the house looking for problems to complain about. The wife, a mother of four, scrubbed and cleaned constantly, as well as held a part-time job at home, but the house was never clean enough. If a child left a toy out, or took a blanket out to make a tent in the backyard, the husband would be disgusted with the mess and let everybody know about it. Within a few minutes of his arrival home, the kids were crying and the wife was upset. Angry and resentful, the children were punished. She had failed again, failed to meet his expectations. Satan was stealing joy from these families and mine too.

In my own case, I was intent on having the best-looking sheep at the fair. I expected my husband to show sheer them because I was afraid I might cut them. Show shearing is similar to ice carving. It takes approximately three to five hours to get every fiber smooth and cut just right. My husband did his best, but if he took a little too much wool off in one area or another, I had a fit. To me, all the work we had done to that point just went down the drain. You cannot put wool back on. I pointed out how careless he had been. He threw his hands up in the air and walked away disgusted. When I finally recognized this enemy called perfectionism, which I had always thought was a good side of me, I was ashamed. I had elevated myself and my ideas above others. Thank God, at least my sheep didn't know the ideals I had set for them. But my family, oh, my poor family, how I had hurt them.

I sat down and wrote a letter to each of my family and released them from my expectations. I love them all just the way they are, and I pray God will mend the broken pieces and wounds I have created.

Recently I saw a program about people who had stage fright. The underlying cause was a significant other in their life who supplied a blow to their ego each time they didn't measure up. A critical spirit binds up those who become victims of it. Soon they are unable to do things like sing out loud, give their opinion, share Jesus with another, or raise their hands in church to worship God, because they are afraid they might do it wrong. Inhibition is a result. It stifles their ability to grow and become the people God wants them to be.

I don't know how perfectionism seems to take over our personalities, but I am grateful that I had a mother who encouraged me, who told me I was beautiful, and who gave me the confidence to be free to express myself. What I thought was a good thing can go too far when it hurts others. There are too many victims suffering from this abuser. I am grateful I understand this lesson now, and I am working hard to see perfectionism put to death in my life.

Jesus is constantly working to make us more like Him. His desire is to see us value others more than ourselves. He needs us to be teachable and open to His guidance, to learn to be a good shepherd to anyone He brings across our paths. He never hid anything but let Himself be open for all to see. I once read a little line that said, "When Jesus returns, He will not be looking for our medals, but for our scars."

If you see this enemy in your personality, confess it as sin. Bind it (Matt. 18:18) and cast it out. Renounce its legal right to be in you. Then ask God to fill you with His grace for others. Then work on changing your ways. An old habit is hard to shake, but when you recognize it and realize how horrible it can be, close the door to it. Let your family know you have recognized you have hurt them with it, and ask their forgiveness. If you notice it trying to come back, get it under your feet. Once you have conquered it, you'll be blessed by a much happier family. You will be free at last.

CHAPTER 13

># FEAR NO EVIL

LIVING IN FEAR IS A TERRIBLE thing. I once read an article that claimed people who live in fear live only half a life. Fear can surely stop, or at least hinder, how God wants to use us. "Perfect love casts out all fear" (1 John 4:18) had always been a verse I could not quite grasp until we met Brian.

My youngest daughter, Lisa, about sixteen at the time, was down at the fairgrounds getting her sheep ready for the show. They require not just taming, but washing. (Judges even look in ears and feel under their tummies where you need to practically turn upside down to clean them.) Sheep also need to be sheered, trimmed, and have their feet clipped. Owners also need to keep the stall and aisle clean at all times.

Lisa was a very pretty girl with long, naturally curly hair that fell down across her shoulders in ringlets. I glanced back at her busily working, marveling at how such a tiny girl could handle such large sheep. I left her there for a while and ran a few errands. Upon my return, I noticed an intimidating-looking young man leaning on a barn post, staring at my daughter. He was about six feet tall and dressed in a black leather jacket and ripped blue jeans. What looked like a knife handle protruded from his scuffed boots.

He looked like he had been in some scraps from the scars on his hands and face. He was definitely not the type of guy you wanted hanging around your daughter.

Lisa seemed uneasy, so I helped her clean up, and we left for home. Apparently he had been there the day before as well when I wasn't around.

He had told her he was part of the carnival crew and was able to spend time with her every day. She didn't know how to get rid of him. We prayed, and a thought came to mind. *We'll share Jesus with him!* Either he won't be able to listen to it and leave, or he'll get saved. Sounded like a good idea to Lisa, so we boldly headed down together the next day.

It was not long before his dark image appeared in the corner of the barn. He walked steadily toward us and let out a grunt in response to our, "Hi, how ya doing?" His blond, greasy hair was perfectly straight. At least he looked like he had run a comb through it.

Lisa mentioned the names of her sheep: Joy, Patience, Praise, etc. He mentioned he had a big black dog once he had named Satan. She told him about her youth group at church going to Mexico. He told us how he hit the pastor at his mom and dad's Mormon church and how he had been thrown out. Finally, I invited him to join us for lunch, figuring he'd probably follow us anyway.

We bought him a hot dog, some fries, and a pop, and we sat down at the end of a long picnic table with several people who were enjoying their meals. He was rather surprised that I had bought him a meal, and settled himself down to enjoy it. "Ever read the Bible?" I spoke up.

"Nah, don't read much 'cept maybe a comic book." He grinned.

"Well, do you like riddles?" I continued as I pulled a small New Testament from my purse.

"Yeah, maybe." He wiped some mustard from his chin with his jacket sleeve.

"Well, listen to this." I started reading from John 1. "'In the beginning was the Word, and the Word was with God, and the Word was God. He was with God in the beginning.'" By this time everyone at the table had stopped eating, their mouths hanging open.

I went on, "So God was not alone in the beginning, right?"

"Yeah." He managed through a mouthful of food.

"'Through him all things were made; without him nothing was made that has been made.'" I read on.

"So the Word and God are one, and they created everything, right?"

Another clearer "Yeah" came from his semi-interested mind.

"'In him was life, and that life was the light of men. The light shines in the darkness, but the darkness has not understood it.' You can see there is a mystery here, can't you, that some don't understand? So the Word is God, and the Word is the light, right?"

Another "Yeah." We were doing good.

"'There came a man who was sent from God; his name was John. He came as a witness to testify concerning that light, so that through him all men might believe. He himself was not the light; he came only as a witness to the light. The true light that gives light to every man was coming into the world.' So God, the Word, the Light, is coming into the world, right?" He only nodded this time, but that was good enough for me.

"'He was in the world, and though the world was made through him, the world did not recognize him. He came to that which was his own, but his own did not receive him. Yet to all who received him, to those who believed in his name, he gave the right to become children of God. Children born not of natural descent, nor of human decision or a husband's will, but born of God.'

"We are not children of God unless we believe in the God who came to our world, then, are we?"

"Nope."

Hey, there is hope here. I can feel it.

No one at our table was chewing except our new friend. I went on. "'The Word became flesh and made his dwelling among us. We have seen his glory, the glory of the One and Only, who came from the Father full of grace and truth. John testifies concerning him. He cries out, saying, "This was he of whom I said, 'He who comes after me has surpassed me because he was before me.'"' Who is the Word?"

"God," he replied.

"Who is the Light?"

"God," he answered again.

"Who is the One and Only who came from the Father?"

"God."

"And He came before John, why?"

"Because He's God," he answered correctly again.

"Now, listen to this: 'From the fullness of his grace we have all received one blessing after another. For the law was given through Moses, grace and truth came through Jesus Christ. No one has ever seen God, but God the One and Only, who is at the Father's side, has made him known.'

"If Jesus is the One and Only, then what is God's name?"

I paused as he reflected a moment.

"Jesus!" he burst out. "Jesus is God." With that, shouts of victory came from not only our table, but all around us as well. Unaware that anyone had been listening, he began grinning. He figured out the riddle. He had done something right.

The next few days we were presented with question after question. We actually looked forward to seeing him each day.

The fair was about to end. We gave our new friend our telephone number and told him to give us a call when he was ready to ask Jesus into his life.

Several weeks went by before we got his call. He was ready and prayed with me over the phone to receive his new life. Several days later, he called again. He wanted to see Lisa. He had something he wanted to show her.

"Well, I am just about to go pick her up at school. How about if I pick you up on the way back, and we'll go have a Coke or something?"

As we pulled into the parking lot where we were to meet him, we couldn't believe our eyes. There he stood dressed in white with a cross around his neck and Bible in hand. Lisa and I looked at each other and smiled. Heaven was smiling too.

CHAPTER 14

SHEEP WORSHIP

LIFE WENT ON AT THE FARM innocently enough. We attended church regularly, prayed, and read our Bibles, but another lesson lurked just ahead of the next turn in the road.

God declares in the Ten Commandments:

> You shall not make for yourself an idol in the form of anything in heaven above or on the earth beneath or in the waters below. You shall not bow down to them or worship them; for I, the Lord your God, am a jealous God, punishing the children for the sin of the fathers to the third and fourth generation of those who hate me, but showing love to a thousand generations of those who love me and keep my commandments. (Exod. 20:4)

Though it is obvious enough to most of us that we are not to make statues and worship them, this verse goes much deeper. God looks at our heart. Love devoted to something we place above God is idol worship. Just as God tested Abram when He commanded him to make a sacrifice of his beloved son, Isaac, God will test us if our hearts start to wander from our first love. Did Abram love his son more than God? No. He passed the test with flying colors. God held first position in his life.

Even though we do wonderful things for Jesus, still He warns us:

> These are the words of him who holds the seven stars in his right hand and walks among the seven golden lampstands: I know your deeds, your hard work and your perseverance. I know that you cannot tolerate wicked men, that you have tested those who claim to be apostles but are not, and have found them false. You have persevered and have endured hardships for my name, and have not grown weary. Yet I hold this against you: You have forsaken your first love. (Rev. 2:1–4)

The Lord often refers to us as His bride. Just like any other bridegroom, He wants the love of His intended. If we scrubbed our mate's floors, fixed his food, and did his laundry faithfully but loved another and our heart was elsewhere, it would devastate our marriage.

Our first love is the Lord, and nothing can come between that love of God and His bride. We may be going along in life quite innocently, thinking everything is fine between God and ourselves, then suddenly God puts His finger on a problem. It is a startling thing when the Lord looks down from heaven and questions you. "Where is your heart?"

Larry, a macho-type guy, stopped by our farm one afternoon to pick out a ram to buy from our flock. He had been a rancher for years and knew his stuff. He picked out from a distance one he seemed interested in. "I'd like to see that one." He pointed at one we had named Judah.

"Com'mere, sweet pea," I called, beckoning him with my hand.

"Sweet pea!" Larry echoed with astonishment. "Don't call him things like that. You're going to make a sissy out of him!"

The lamb came up to see what I might have for him, and Larry examined him carefully. "Looks sound," he said. "How much ya want for him?"

I told him, and he tried to bargain me down, but I stuck to my guns. We loaded him into Larry's pickup, and then Larry asked where he could rinse his hands. I led him over to our hose and turned on the water for him.

"What's this," again with surprise, "you got warm water coming out of your hose?"

"Well," I replied, "you don't think I'd wash my sheep in cold water, do you?"

I'm sure Larry made a real stud out of our little ram and probably renamed him something like Rambo.

I often called my lambs *sweet pea* or *sugar* or *love bug*— endearing little names. My granddaughter once asked if sweet pea was a Bible name.

I even sang to them in the barn, songs such as, "Ewe must have been a beautiful baby."

I had my neighbor girl convinced that the reason my lambs were bigger than hers was because I sang to them every day.

It grew hard for me to sell my sheep to some people. They had a good, clean, and loving home with us, and I hated to see them sold to someone who would fence them into a mud sty and neglect them. I reviewed with buyers how to care for their sheep, giving them a paper of detailed instructions on what to do when. I even bought a stack of books so I could give one to each person who bought a sheep from me. *A Shepherd Looks at Psalm 23*, by Phillip Keller, emphasized the importance of being a *good* shepherd. Still, I struggled with the sale of a lamb, particularly when someone wanted to buy another because the first one died.

I enjoyed my sheep. I loved my sheep; they were part of my family. I took great pleasure in the time I spent with them. Then one day the pastor at our church taught a message on Matthew 6:19–21.

> Do not store up for yourselves treasures on earth, where moth and rust destroy, and where thieves break in and steal. But store up for yourselves treasures in heaven, where moth and rust do not destroy, and where thieves do not break in and steal. For where your treasure is there your heart will be also.

The pastor this particular day had us think about where most of our time was being spent each day. It was summer, and I had been spending a lot of time with my sheep—getting them ready for the fair, watering their pastures, feeding them, petting them as I walked by, talking to them as I pulled thistles from their pasture.

Guilt started creeping in, and then the big question: Was I making an idol out of my sheep? Was I loving them more than God? It was all I could do to pull myself up out of my seat at the end of the service and go forward to repent of my sin.

Questions raced through my head. Did I need to give them up? *Could* I give them up? Were they too important to me? I went home that Sunday, torn apart by the seriousness of the matter.

Several months back I had been preparing to go to King County Jail to share the good news with the inmates there. God had given me that same verse then. "Store up for yourselves treasures in heaven."

He made it clear to me that those men in jail were my treasures as well as His. He was starting to show me how I needed to transfer that love I had for my sheep to people.

That night my daughter and I walked through several sections of security compartments and finally joined four men who were to minister to about twenty-five inmates. We were informed not to touch them or give them anything. We were not to tell them our full names or ask theirs. We had been searched, fingerprinted, and required to leave all our belongings—such as purse and driver's license—at the front desk. We stood there in a plain, cold room with a half circle of chairs as the men filed in.

There were several black men; five or six white men; one big Native American, who stood in a corner with his arms folded in front of him rather than join the others; a few Hispanics; and two men who looked like they could have been my bankers.

We all grouped into a circle as one of the pastors led us in a few songs. Several knew the songs well and happily sang along. A good break from a dull day, I presumed. But not the big Indian in the corner, who reminded me a lot of the Indian in the movie, *One Flew Over the Cuckoo's Nest*. His eyes stared straight ahead. His attitude seemed to be full of resentment and hatred.

Some started improvising their own verses to one of the familiar songs we were singing, but they were anything but familiar to my twenty-year-old daughter and me. "No more crack cocaine, we're going to see the King!" Lisa and I exchanged surprised looks and then joined in the chorus.

Finally it was my turn to share. I read the verse God had given me for that night about storing up your treasures in heaven and how I had questioned God about that verse.

"What treasures am I to store up here on earth, Lord?" I asked Him innocently.

"What goes to heaven?" He replied to me.

"People do." I sometimes wonder how God has such patience with us; we are so brilliant.

I looked around the room of faces. Many looked ready to hear, "You're going to hell, you sinner." But instead I began, "Do you know that to God, you are a treasure?" Even the Indian seemed to be taken off guard. It was God's message to them. He loved them no matter what, and God made a difference to them that night.

By the time the message was over, and Lisa had sung several songs about how Jesus had given His life for them, the evening had become one of the most memorable times of my life. One Hispanic, the two men who looked like they could have been bankers, and the wonderful Indian man gave their lives to Jesus. Lisa nudged my shoulder and brought my attention to the tear trickling down the weather-beaten face of our big man in the corner, who no longer had his arms folded across his chest. Oh, how we longed to throw our arms around them and welcome them into the Lord's family. We could not, but we will in heaven when we meet again someday.

God in His great mercy did not cause me to suffer long about giving up my sheep. Once I had decided that if they were more important to me than God, I would give them up, the floodgates opened. God said to me, "Just as you are created for My pleasure, so I created them for your pleasure. I take joy in your joy. You too are My treasure."

CHAPTER 15

⚬

IN A RUT?

HAVE YOU EVER SEEN A PATH in the woods that deer walk on? Sheep do the same thing. They show up at the same place, at the same feeder, every day and sit in the same place in the same pew. Oops, I didn't mean to get so personal.

They also have trouble making new friends.

There are several kinds of ruts that sheep can get themselves into. The rut aforementioned is a *habit rut*. Next we will examine a case of what we might call a *social rut*.

We once purchased eight sheep from a show and sale in Colorado. We let them out with the others when we got home; but each time we looked out the window, there were our sheep, and then there were the eight others in a different area.

This went on for months, until one day we sheared them all. Suddenly, no one could recognize anyone. Stripped of their fine coats, their pride, and their confidence, they all fought for leadership positions until finally we had one flock. There is always a leader in the group, and if she happens to be the one that knows how to open your gate, or crawl under your fence, you have real problems.

As trust builds for their shepherd, sheep eagerly come at your call. If you open a gate into a fresh area for them to graze in, they don't hesitate for an instant to go on to greener pastures. God wants us to trust Him like that. How many gates has He opened for us and we have questioned whether we should go or not. How many greener pastures have we missed out on because they were out of our comfort zone, or basically our "self-imposed rut."

Now let's look at a *fear-induced rut*. I often thought Adam got confused when he named them sheep. A better name would be chickens. Sheep are afraid of their shadow. They can be dying of thirst but won't go to the creek for a drink of water unless accompanied by another. I guess that is understandable, though, knowing that they are completely defenseless. They will also avoid grazing in an area of greener grass because of fear of what might be hiding behind a tree. Fear can be overcome, however, if they remain in sight of their shepherd.

One beautiful sunny afternoon I thought I would let them out behind our house into the forested area where lots of tender long grass had grown. They eagerly followed me, knowing I had a special treat for them in the woods. I had to tiptoe away or they would have followed me out again. I went about 100 feet into my backyard, where I began raking leaves.

Suddenly, a twig snapped. Woolly heads popped up, ears alert, as they looked everywhere until they caught my eye. The pounding of hooves headed straight for me.

I was sure I was dead meat, with each of my twenty-five woolly friends weighing approximately 300 pounds, but at the last minute they swerved behind me and stopped. There, they peered back around me into the woods to see what the noise was, as though I would surely protect them from anything that might be after them. And they were right. No matter what had come out of those woods, it would have had to face me and my rake before it would have had my sheep. They were adorable and certainly knew how to make me feel needed. Like my sheep, we too can feel safe, for our shepherd, Jesus, is watching over us, and He has more than a rake to defend us with.

Have you ever noticed how independence can be a rut? Sometimes I think it would be better if we were more like sheep, never wanting our Savior out of our sight. How much more we would receive if we were just willing to admit our defenselessness and our great need for Him.

I have many little lambs that will come up to me and nibble a little grain out of my hand. But if I reach out to pet them, or try to hold them in my arms, they run off. They are independent, happy, and loved, but they don't know what they are missing. The lamb that is born weak, the one that is sick or crippled, or the one that is rejected and needs me is the one I am able to spend time with. I will carry this little lamb and lay with him in the field. I will be his shade on a hot day. I will gladly see to his every need. I will enjoy him, and our love grows much deeper than with the lamb I cannot hold. But, alas, even when we do lose sight of our Shepherd, He does not lose sight of us.

Sheep have been known to fall into a *most serious rut*. Star was a lamb born on Christmas day. We named him after the star of Bethlehem that once shone over another lamb in another manger long ago. He was nearly twenty pounds at birth, and his rate of gain was fantastic. He was going to be a champion.

It had been an exceptionally wet winter. Flooding had happened in many of the major rivers around Snohomish. It was April now, and the showers had done their job. Everything was green and growing. Our little creek in the middle of the pasture had swelled from its usual one foot across, to two feet and overflowed in areas.

My husband and I had been in town at the vet's with a lamb that needed some minor surgery. It was dark by the time we got home, and she was anxious to get back to her mother. I heard a ewe making a lot of noise in the back of the barn. I took the little lamb out to her, but suddenly realized it was not her mother causing all the commotion, but Star's mother. She was under a shelter, staring out into the darkness, calling her son. He was calling back to her. He sounded weak. Urgency gripped my heart. While I hurried blindly off into the darkness, my husband tried to find a flashlight.

I had to go only on sound because the night was very dark, but I could tell I was getting close. Aware that I was at the creek bed, I knelt down to feel for him. Lower and lower I felt until finally I found his head, the only part of him that was above water. I reached into the ice-cold water and tried to pull his little legs free from the mud. The raging waters had dug a ditch nearly three feet deep. It was only about ten inches wide. Somehow he had fallen in and gotten himself stuck in it.

I got his front two legs free but could not pull him all the way out. He weighed over a hundred pounds with the wet wool and mud. My husband finally arrived and helped get him out the rest of the way. We set him on his feet, but he could not walk. He tried but fell to the ground. Alan hurriedly went back for a wheelbarrow, and we wheeled him to the house, where we lifted him into the laundry tub in the basement and began filling it with very warm water. It took forty-five minutes for him to quit shivering. He didn't try to struggle with us at all but actually fell asleep with my hand supporting his little head, the rest of his body totally submerged in steaming water.

When we felt he was safely warm enough, we lifted him out. With a big blow drier we use on our show sheep, we dried him off then returned him to the barn, where he immediately found some dinner under his worried mother's rear leg.

The mother's cries for her young one got the shepherd's attention, but he would not have been found in the dark unless he called out also. It is the same with us and our parents. They may pray and get God's attention, but there is little else they can do. Sometimes no one can help us out of our rut except our Shepherd. But when we are in the darkness of sin, there is nothing our Shepherd can do for us until we cry out for His help ourselves.

Sometimes we find ourselves stuck in such a rut, cold and unable to walk. Instead of looking at the mud around you, cry out to the Lord. He will come to your rescue. Spend time with Him. Let Him warm you. If you keep a journal of the times Jesus has helped you in the past, read it. Revisit the arms of love that want to hold you. Listen to some favorite songs of adoration and rest. Soon you will be on your feet again, back with the others, hungry for life again.

God can get us out of just about any rut we get ourselves into if we are willing to let Him. But sometimes we just need to recognize our rut and do something about it.

Are you in a rut? Do you want to serve God? Then volunteer. God will be there and supply all you need. When I was asked to be the president of the ministry chapter, I had never even been on a board. I had no idea of how things worked. Then God gave me a picture and a verse. The verse was that Israel would bud and blossom. I took that to mean the group I would be ministering to would grow and come to maturity. The vision was of me standing in a patch of dirt. I had no hoe, no rake, no seeds. But as I needed them, God supplied everything. I found it one of the most growing experiences of my life.

We don't need to *feel* called; we are called. Called to be servants, called to give the good news, called to heal the sick, called to disciple the younger. Do you feel like you don't know enough? There is nothing like experience for growth. It is an adventure waiting with a testimony to follow. We know a lamb is healthy if it stands and stretches when it wakes up. Keep your Shepherd in sight and *stretch.*

CHAPTER 16

LIKE A LAMB TO
THE SLAUGHTER

I HAD OFTEN HEARD messages of Jesus coming into the world humbly, born in a stable. Why not a humble shack? Why in a manger with animals? Why were shepherds the first ones to hear the news and come to the manger to see the newborn Christ child? These are questions I had pondered in my heart.

All through the Old Testament, God had called for a lamb to be sacrificed for sin. Not just any lamb, but a perfect lamb—one without blemish.

When Adam and Eve disobeyed God, an animal—probably a lamb—was killed to cover their sin. When Cain and Abel offered their sacrifices, God accepted Abel's lamb and rejected Cain's offering of fruits and vegetables. Why? Because He wanted to point the way to the Lamb of God, who would take away the sins of the world.

Zoanne Wilkie a speaker at our womens group brought the revelation of the answer. Jesus had to be born in a stable. That's where lambs are born, and that's why shepherds had to be in attendance. God wanted us to recognize that

Jesus was that promised lamb that He had been pointing to all throughout history. Jesus was to be the lamb sacrificed in the prime of His life. He had to be without blemish, or sin free, to be an acceptable sacrifice. Only God could do this, and in His love He sent this precious lamb to us, His only Son.

We all know that fear is not from God, and that perfect love casts out all fear. Yet even our Savior, in His human form, sweated drops of blood as He prayed to His Father, "My father, if it is possible, may this cup be taken from me. Yet not as I will, but as you will" (Matt. 26:39).

In other words, "Father, if there is any other way to restore mankind to God, set Me free from the torture and death that You have asked Me to endure." But there was no other way for man in his sin to be forgiven and placed in a relationship again with God the Father.

While in Israel, I noticed in the Garden of Gethsemane in Jerusalem the ancient olive trees that are twisted and gnarled as if in agony, as if they had experienced the pain Jesus felt that day long ago. There was also only one type of flower growing there at the time. A blood-red poppy. They are scattered all over Israel. Their petals are the shape of a drop of blood. It is as if He left them as a reminder of the hard choice He had to make that day to give Himself for us. Jesus had to be crucified. Jesus knew all the pain we know as humans, yet He had allowed Himself to be led like a sheep to the slaughter. Just as sheep put total trust in their shepherd, He placed total trust in His Father.

When we realize that death is just a doorway to eternity, and we know our Shepherd is there waiting for us, we can go through even the valley of death without fear.

Before we were Christians, and when my second child was only six weeks old, I became pregnant again. I was not aware of this pregnancy until I was about four to five months along. I saw the doctor because I was gaining weight, not losing. The news was not what I wanted to hear. My other child was going on two. I could not picture having three children under the age of two and a half all in diapers, and a husband who drove cabs at night and slept in the day.

My mother suggested jumping off the kitchen counter and taking hot mustard baths. I tried both, but the pregnancy continued. Just when I was resigned to this new development, I became very sick. I was about six months along. I went in for my usual checkup, telling the doctor I could not keep anything down and I felt awful.

He listened intently for a heartbeat. He could hear none. Then he asked me if I had felt any movement. When I answered no, we looked at each other eye to eye, both suspecting the worst.

"I'm afraid your baby is dead and is poisoning your system."

The words pounded in my head. I had killed my baby. Guilt poured over me. Suddenly, I was not only physically sick but also sick at heart.

"We'll need to admit you into the hospital immediately."

Within a couple of hours I was lying on a hospital bed, and my husband was by my side as we waited for the contractions to start. They were putting some kind of clear liquid into me intravenously, and I would start labor at any time. The minutes turned into hours, and the hours slowly crept by, yet nothing happened.

That evening the doctor came in to see me. He listened again to my swollen abdomen and looked puzzled. He had a couple of nurses wheel my bed into another room where they affixed a lot of wires to my tummy, and then turned a machine on to check what was happening. They had done something wrong in hooking it up and gave me quite a shock. They changed a few wires and tried again. Much to all of our surprise, they recorded two tiny heartbeats from two tiny babies. They were alive, and I was going to be the mother of four children under two and a half. Tears of relief trickled down my cheeks as I watched those two little hearts rhythmically beating along.

I was sent home that night with instructions to take it easy for a few days. My husband and I had a lot to think about, but I was still so ill and weak that I soon fell fast asleep.

In the morning, my husband set up the playpen next to my bed and made sure everything he could think of was near me. Mark was still asleep in his crib in the other room, but he was able to get out and come see mamma by himself. Then Alan left for work. I was nursing my little one, so I would not have to get up to fix bottles. Shortly after my husband had left, I had to get up to go to the bathroom.

Suddenly there was a burst of water mixed with blood. I pulled myself up to the bathroom window and started yelling for help. Soon the whole neighborhood was in my house, trying to figure out what to do with me. At first, I was nearly incoherent and unable to communicate clearly who my doctor was or how to reach my husband. I was shaking all over and hemorrhaging profusely.

Finally we got my doctor's office on the phone. After several minutes they told them to bring me in. It was about a forty-five minute drive to his office. When we arrived, we found he had meant for us to go to the hospital, not the clinic. So we wound up with another thirty-minute drive. Even though I was lying in the back seat, I was losing blood seemingly by the buckets.

They told me at the hospital they would not be able to give me any drugs, because I would have to remain awake to help deliver the babies that were transversal, or criss-crossed across each other. But I must have passed out because suddenly I woke up in the ICU. My arm ached from having cold blood pumped into me. I looked up at the tubes running into my arm and then noticed a young man with curly blond hair lying next to me. Apparently they had run out of blood at the hospital, and this young man was giving me his blood direct.

I remember looking up at the ceiling, and then suddenly I was no longer in my body. I was falling down, down, down while I was looking up at the back of my body. I remember my reaction vividly. "They must have given me drugs. This must be what they call *hallucinating*. They said they would not give me any drugs." I was definitely upset at this, as I had purposely avoided taking drugs my whole life.

Down and down I continued, still lying in the same position, yet there was my body above me. I was dead, but I did not know it. I was headed for hell, but I did not realize it.

I often thought afterward how everyone who had shared death experiences had drifted up above their bodies. Why had I gone down? It made no sense to me until I was born again, and I realized that I had only known about God. Now I *knew* Him. God knew my future, and even though Satan tried to snatch my life before I found Jesus, God was there to give me another chance.

My babies were born dead, two little boys we named Adam and Aaron. They weighed one pound, eight ounces and one pound, twelve ounces.

Years later, I was at a retreat listening to a lady tell about her nine-year-old son who was killed in a terrible car accident. He knew Jesus and loved to tell people about Him.

One day, many years later, she was pondering in her heart if her little boy grew up in heaven or remained a child. Suddenly, the Lord gave her a vision. She saw a magnificent white stallion with his muscles taught, pawing the ground with main flying in the wind. Upon his back, she saw a young man dressed in armor. It was her son. He looked about nineteen.

As she talked, I saw two more horses standing behind and to the sides of the one she was describing. As I looked up their beautiful muscular legs, I saw two young men who looked extremely familiar. They looked so healthy, so strong, so pure. My focus remained on their faces until suddenly it hit me: They were my boys, Adam and Aaron. They would have been about twenty-nine then. They had known no sin, no disease, no corruption. They were poised, ready for the signal to come and take their mamma home. The sight of them brought such relief and joy, I can hardly tell the story without tears coming to my eyes. Our Savior is so kind and thoughtful, and it is so wonderful to have His reassurance that some day we will be together again.

Another episode with death showed me how our dear Lord still serves us with lovingkindness. My mother passed away a few days before Mother's Day in 1985. She and I were very close; I was a late-in-life child, and my father died when I was only eight. The family, knowing it would be a hard day for me to get through, chose to spend Mother's Day with me at my home. They brought lots of things to eat, and the last of them left about 8:00 P.M.

That night as I sat on my bed with my Bible on my lap, I was feeling rather sad because the only thing I didn't get to do was put flowers on my mother's grave. I glanced down to where my hand was resting on my open Bible.

"Ask anything in my name and it shall be done for you."

My wonderful Savior was speaking to my hurting heart.

"Would You take my mother some roses and tell her I love her?" I replied, and I know He did.

Jesus was led like a lamb to the slaughter so that we and our loved ones could be together again, together with Him in paradise. When my grandfather died, he exclaimed to my grandmother, "Look, Sarah! Do you see Him?

"Who, John? Who do you see?"

"It's Jesus, and He's beautiful."

CHAPTER 17

⁂

FLOCK ANIMALS

WHENEVER WE SELL A SHEEP to someone, we always try to sell them two. Not because we want to sell more sheep, but because we know they need companionship. They are miserable when alone.

Each year our church had a wonderful live nativity scene performance. A darling donkey carried Mary, pregnant with child, to the town of Bethlehem. There the innkeeper shook his head and pointed toward the stable. Llamas disguised as camels accompanied the three kings to see the Christ child. We took a few of our sheep to be part of the drama.

They wanted us to tie one lamb to a fence just outside the manger, across from the donkey. The rest were put out in a field with the shepherds about thirty feet away. We gave them all some alfalfa to keep them happy and settle them down for the three, half-hour performances in which they were to participate. The lights dimmed except for the amber glow coming from the manger. The angels on the rooftop stopped their dancing, and all actors froze as if in a picture on a Christmas card. The star of Bethlehem shone high in the sky as "Silent Night, Holy Night" played softly in the background. Everything was incredibly beautiful and peaceful. Until, that is, my lamb tied by the fence noticed she was alone.

Suddenly she cried out, "Baa," which was returned immediately by the other sheep. "Baa." Then, excitedly she "baaed" again, and they nervously returned the call. Then without warning she jumped the fence. But being short-tied, she merely flipped herself over. She was lying on the manger side, upside down, kicking all feet frantically in the air and making all sorts of noise. What a mess! We got her untied and put another lamb alongside her. No more problems. I really hoped they caught that on video. I know I would have won the prize for the funniest video.

As president of a ladies' organization, I saw many women who had lost their mate and were very lonely. Part of them was missing, and it really could not be replaced.

Perhaps I feel for them because I was raised as an only child. My two sisters were both married by the time I was a year and a half old. With no siblings to play with, loneliness had played a role in my life. It is more common than one might expect, and even in a crowd of people we can feel left out and alone.

Many years ago I decided to go to my first Christian women's conference in Florida. The chapter I belonged to had several ladies who went every year, and they always came back raving about the wonderful time they had. Husbands were welcome to join their wives, so I invited my daughter and husband along. But the three of us were quite unsure of what to expect, even though we were given a packet of information upon arrival.

We flew on a different flight than the rest of the girls and were staying at a different hotel because we had booked later than they had. When we finally saw them, I felt assured they would lead us in what to do when. But I failed to verbalize my need, and they, thinking I was with my husband and daughter, thought there was no need to keep in touch with us. Try as I may each day, I could not seem to find my friends in the vast numbers of people. The conferences hold anywhere from 10,000 to 15,000 women and about 500 men.

Whenever I did find our group, they had already eaten or there were no extra seats saved for the three of us. I was struggling with rejection and hurt so much that grumbling had set in. Instead of having a wonderful time, I started resenting those other women. I was so down by the final day that I didn't even want to go hear Joni Erickson-Tada, the last speaker. I felt a paraplegic could have nothing to share that I would be able to relate to. After all, she had a handicap, and I was perfectly able to get around.

Finally I decided to make one last attempt by saving seven extra seats and then searching frantically for them before the meeting. They joined us at last, and we were able to visit for a short time before the meeting began. But then, halfway through the message, they got up to leave. When I questioned where they were going, one of them called back. They had rented a van, and they were going shopping.

My husband, knowing my let down, took my hand. My daughter put her arm around me, but their efforts could not stop the pain I felt. I turned my attention to what the speaker was sharing. Joni told us how totally helpless she was, and how she needed constant attention because of bed-sores she would get and not be aware of. She had no feeling in most of her body, so she was unaware of the sores that could easily lead to infection and become life threatening if not attended to.

As a result of a swimming accident, she had been an invalid since she was seventeen years old. She had missed the dances, the prom, the dates, the ability to drive, to have children, and to even turn over in bed, yet she was thanking God for her condition. She said that she spent hours daily with Jesus. Dwelling in His arms, listening to His heartbeat, hearing His voice. She had found something in life much more precious than all the things I had. She had a depth of relationship and love of her Savior that few achieve. Then she said, "If I had legs, I would have missed so much. Instead of all this wonderful time I have spent with my Savior, I would probably have gone shopping."

Tears flowed down my cheeks. I did have a handicap. We all do, whether it be physical or emotional. Here among 10,000 women, God knew my pain and spoke the words through Joni that I needed to hear. I didn't go shopping. I heard God's loving message instead.

After the sermon, we decided to go to the hotel pool. There at the hot tub sat a lonely young man from England. He shared openly with me that he was on vacation to try to get over a relationship of six years. His girlfriend suddenly married another man, just after he had bought a ring and was preparing to ask her to marry him. His heart had been broken. God arranged to have me there to comfort him and tell him the good news of the One who would never let him down. That young man gave his life to Jesus that day by the pool. Sometimes Jesus has a reason for keeping us separate from the others. He had a lost lamb He had to show the way home.

There are times when Jesus comforts and even uses our loneliness, but Satan often singles out a lost lamb to devour. If I had left that meeting early and not heard the message, I could have harbored bitterness and resentment for years. We need friends, and we need to make our needs known. We also need to be sensitive to others.

Ask God for the gift of hospitality if you are feeling lonely. Be the one who invites, who comforts, who loves. What you sow, you will reap. If you feel intimidated at first, ask for prayer to overcome it, and then walk it out. Go home and ask someone over. One bold step can conquer that enemy.

CHAPTER 18

WRONG FLOCK

JESUS TELLS A PARABLE OF THE LOST SHEEP, and how the Good Shepherd leaves the ninety and nine to go after the one that has strayed. It is said that the shepherds of Israel would retrieve a lost lamb once or twice, but if it is a habitual wanderer, the shepherd will break it's legs and carry it over his shoulders until the relationship is cemented, and the sheep is healed of broken limb, and of wandering. It is much better for the lamb than being lost forever, or eaten by a wolf. Our son was attending a College and Career group at our church with his sister, yet on Good Friday one year, he decided to go to a party with the guys from his construction job instead. I tried unsuccessfully to persuade him that this was Good Friday, and he should spend time with other Christian young people. I suspected the party he was going to attend there would be drinking and possibly drugs. He did his best to convince me that he would not drink, and that he would even try to tell some of them about Jesus.

At five in the morning he returned, his nose broken, his lip cut, his eye blackened, and his wallet missing. It seems when he noticed his wallet was gone at the party, he shut off the music to ask if anyone had seen it. Someone was dancing and got perturbed that Mark had shut off the music. He promptly turned it back on before Mark had a chance to say anything. So Mark shut it off again, only to find himself attacked by more than one angry man.

The next morning there was a dialogue on the radio between two Christian young men. One was saying that another man had lied to him, and then had made him look like the bad guy, and finally stole his girlfriend. He said " I was so mad at him that I could just hauled off and ....prayed for him."

"That is the flock of sheep we belong to," I told Mark. When we turn and go back to old lifestyle patterns we open a door to Satan's attack. We learn by consequence, as God's heart breaks over our bad decisions to go back to Egypt. But our son did not seem to learn. He kept relationships going with drug users and continued to lead what we felt was a self destructive life.

The idea of being in the wrong flock doesn't mean we are not to spend time with the unsaved. Jesus dined with sinners knowing it was they who needed Him the most. But we need to be healed before we go back into an area that might cause temptation and pull us back into Satan's trap. In order to be a good witnesses to them we must do as Jesus directs in Matthew 16:24-28 *"If anyone would come after me, he must deny himself and take up his cross and follow me."* We must deny ourselves the "pleasures" of our pasts that only lead to destruction, and pick up the new life. We must value the new life the Lord has provided for us, and treasure the second chance. The cross is not an easy one to carry, but the rewards along life's path are worth it all, as we learn to listen to His voice and obey Him.

Over a period of about fifteen years, we took Mark in five times. We cared about him and couldn't stand seeing him through his life away. We would get him off drugs for a few months, back on his feet, and then he would leave. He would last a week or two, and then pivot back into his old habits. I kept telling him "Mark, when you leave the nest, you are supposed to flap your wings."

Things got worse and worse each time he came back. My husband and I had been taking a break from ministering, we were just attending church for several weeks, and spending most of our time working on the farm. We had not prayed much, or spent much time reading our Bible. We decided to start praying for an hour each morning before we got out of bed. We said simple little prayers like "Dear Lord, please keep our son safe," and "Lord help him to keep out of bad company." We had no idea what he was involved with at the time.

Mark had borrowed money on quite a few of those credit cards they send you that offer 6% interest or less, so he could remodel a house he was trying to buy on a lease option, and sell Amway. He was living on the money, and thought he would hit it big in this multi marketing business. He bought every tape they put out, went to every seminar, and had a room full of self help books. At least he was dressing better, and seemed to have hope. But as reality settled in, the credit companies suddenly wanted twenty three percent interest, and there was no way he could pay it back. He worked for two years plumbing trying to make up for his debt, but it just kept growing. That's when he turned to gambling and cocaine.

My husband and I had been praying for nine days, when my husband prayed "Lord we haven't shared you with anyone for such a long time, just bring someone up our driveway that needs Jesus." At two in the morning up our driveway came Mark. He limped into our room extremely paranoid. He thought a gang was after him, and would come up our driveway any minute to kill us all. He looked like a 6 foot tall skeleton with skin on. His eyes were hollow, and he was shaking and crying. My husband and I were still in bed. I held my arms out to him, and he collapsed into them.

"Oh mom," he cried out, " I've been doing terrible things. These people mom, they are wicked. They are evil, and they are going to kill us all. We need to call the police."

He nearly had us both convinced. I held him in my arms I told him we were going to turn them over to Jesus instead. We prayed and asked Jesus to hide us from them, to camouflage our drive way, so they could not find us. I felt his body relax in my arms, as we prayed for these people's redemption.

We had quite a night with him. He was out of his mind, shivering and perspiring. We could not seem to keep him warm. We called the local hospital emergency room. They told us to keep him home and just wait it through with him. It was frightening. It was hell. We thought he was going to die he looked so terrible.

He had been with a group of drug dealers who had him on cocaine for nine days straight with nothing to eat, and little to drink. He was dehydrated, and shaking all over.

He was being initiated, he said. He figured that selling drugs was the only way he could pay his debts off. These men took turns driving him around town, sending him in to different stores to cash checks for over the amount of purchases, so he could get enough cash to "buy in."

When the bills started coming in we found he had written $7000.00 in bad checks over the nine day period.

After he was coherent again we realized that he had been with this group the same nine days we had been praying for him. When he finally broke loose from them, he heard God tell him to go home. We took him to the doctor two days later to find he was very dehydrated, and had phenomena. They said his hip was dislocated that is why he was limping.

We went to hear a sermon that following week about Jacob wrestling with God. Jacob came away with a dislocated hip too.

We thought surely this would be the bottom for Mark. This time when he left the nest, he would fly, but no. A short time later he was back on drugs and gambling. There seemed to be no end to it. We could not understand why we could not seem to reach him, why he continued to make such bad choices.

We took him to a Cleansing Stream seminar with us where they discussed the symptoms of a person suffering from a spirit of rejection. Mark fit them all. He went forward for deliverence, but we saw no change. We had always loved him. We could not understand where this spirit had come from.

He disappeared for a while. We tried desperately to find him for three weeks, because we had bought an airline ticket for him to go to a conference with us in New Orleans. He came in at midnight. We were to leave at three a.m. He was a mess, and obviously not able to drive safely. He said he didn't want to go to the conference with us. Somehow by the grace of God, we were able to talk him into going to a drug detox center. As we were driving him there he started screaming "What do you do with something you don't want? You kick it out, you through it away, you put it in the basement."

Suddenly everything fell into place and we understood what had tormented our son for so long. We needed to talk with him, but it was not possible right then. When we came back a few days later, he was gone. We were afraid he was mad at us for leaving him in such a place, but no matter where we tried, we could not find him. We were leaving for a six month mission trip to Hawaii on the fourth of December, and had no idea where he was. We needed to talk with him desperately, but as the clock ticked away, and time ran out there was nothing we could do except pray and leave him a letter. God had revealed the problem to us.

Sometimes, as in my son's case, there are wounds from childhood that keep us from being able to feel worthy of God's love. In Mark's case we brought a new baby home from the hospital when he was five years old. The baby, just as all babies do, got a lot of the attention. But the big blow to him came when we moved him out of his bedroom with his four year old sister and put the new baby in his place, and then made a new room for him in the basement. We had no idea of the consequences he would struggle with because of our actions. He had nightmares he hadn't told us about. He wet the bed nightly because he was afraid to get up. We had no idea what was going on. We thought boys were just more difficult to potty train. We thought the new arrangements were better for him because he had started school, and needed the quiet. We thought he would feel grown up getting his very own room all to himself. It was a lovely room, and we decorated it with lots of little boy things, but we had no idea how he felt.

When he screamed out to us. What do you do with something you don't want? You throw them away. You step on them, you kick them, you put them in the basement!" It all came together.

Our son had been tormented for years because of a mistake we made when he was five years old. He could not fit in with Christians. How could he, he could not even fit in with his family. We have always loved him, but he could not receive that love because of a lie Satan had put into his heart that night when he was little. A lie that grew bigger and bigger with each scolding. A lie that said he was not wanted.

We had learned at the Cleansing Stream seminar about the way people react when under the influence of a spirit of rejection are by being rebellious, resentful, they live in self pity and fear, withdrawal, insecurity and depression. Our poor son had run the gambit. He could not have peace. He could not love or feel loved. He went from revenge and anger to hatred and blame to self hatred.

We did everything in our power to try to help him, but he could not receive. We needed the key to set the captive free. We had to find what had originally caused such pain. Little children are so susceptible to Satan's lies. If it is not detected early it can destroy a whole family.

In January Mark finally surfaced. He had lost everything. His house, his job, his money, and when his van broke down, someone towed it away. He had been sleeping in it, and had no money to get it back. He had twenty six cents when he finally called his sister collect. She picked him up, and put him in contact with us. I told him about the letter I had left for him with his Christmas present, and that we would arrange to have him join us as soon as we could. He sat in our empty house for three days reading my letter, and his Bible. I told him how sorry we were that we had done that to him as a little boy. We didn't realize how he had been hurt. I told him I wish I could hold him in my arms and tell him how terribly sorry we were.

God arranged me to be the speaker at the Church in Hawaii, when our son arrived the first week. I gave my testimony of how I wanted to be the world's best mommie, and how I could not do it without Jesus. I had failed as a mother. But Jesus was changing my heart and my ways. Mark was healing.

Mark had walked forward for prayer at the conference about rejection. He recognized it too, but afterwards we had seen no noticable changes in him. God was at work though. Shortly after he arrived in Hawaii he had a dream. In the dream a man came to him, and wrote down on a piece of paper all the things Mark would have to do in order to be happy. Then the man nailed the paper to a tree. As Mark reached for the paper, it disappeared. Then the man disappeared as well. He awoke from the dream upset that he couldn't read the paper with the instructions on it to his happiness. The interpretation of the dream came through a friend a few days later. The man in the dream was Satan. He made a list of works Mark would have to perform in order to be happy, but when he nailed them to the cross, they disappeared because Jesus had already done everything for him. God was ministering healing our son ravished life.

After a month of rest and some prayers from two Pastors we knew, Mark started to get back on his feet. He has left the drug scene, and has a clean slate. There were no jobs in Hawaii, but Mark got one that paid about twenty five dollars an hour as a journeyman plumber. He had no references, but he got a fully furnished apartment in Waikiki. He prayed for a girlfriend, and God told him to fish on the other side of the boat. He asked a girl out at church, she is wonderful. He asked her to marry him three days before we were to go back home. She said yes! Only God could do all this.

That night we went out dancing at one of the nicer hotels to celebrate. The band announced their engagement, and asked them if they would dance a special dance together. The music they played was "I believe that I can fly." Mark looked over Marie's shoulder to see the tears running down his mother's face. God had let me know. This time my son was going to fly.

If you are feeling like a good parent yet your child is demonstrating hatred, anger, jealousy, fear, bed wetting, reventge-any continual problems you can't understand—try going back to when a little brother or sister was added to the family. Divorce can have the same effect on a child. See if a personality change came about then. Sit with them, pray with them. Be concerned. Don't let Satan get a hold on them. Explain that the devil planted a lie in their hearts when the new child came home from the hospital, or when daddy had to leave. This lie told them they were no longer loved as much as they were before the traumatic event. We need to tell that lie to leave. Anger, hatred, rejection and jealousy must leave in the name of Jesus.

Then tell them we need to fill that place with the Holy Spirit so there is no room for them to come back again. The Holy Spirit consists of love, joy, peace, patience, goodness, faithfulness, kindness, gentleness, and self-control. Take back the life Satan would like to destroy. With an older child sometimes it helps for them to see it again with adult eyes. Go over the details of the event, reassuring them that they were always loved and that God was always with them.

The songs our young people are singing right now are cries of pain. Don't get mad at them when they rebel. They are hurting. The truth can set them free. Help them see it, pray the lie out, and help them forgive.

Keep praying for them. Don't give up. Jesus is praying with you.

CHAPTER 19

THE LIFTER OF MY HEAD

IT IS A THING OF BEAUTY to watch an animal and its owner work together, whether it be a horse leaping magnificently over hurdles or a sheep groomed and trained for the fair. Just as a horseman can control a horse by a slight nudge of a knee, a shepherd is able to present his animal to the judge by holding one hand under its chin. The arm is extended and the hand is gently placed there palm up. Unless the sheep is having a mood problem, the sheep is then totally in the control of the shepherd. It will walk when led forward and stop just like a dog does with its master. With slight adjustment from the shepherd, it will put all four feet in correct positions to be judged. With a little pressure from a knee in its chest, it will tense its muscles, hold its head high and its back straight, and stand confidently, looking glorious and giving honor to its master. It is interesting that there is a verse in the Bible that pertains to just about everything we do with our sheep. Psalm 3:3 reads: "But you are a shield around me, O Lord; you bestow glory on me and lift up my head." (See picture back cover)

Discouragement and low self-esteem can cause us to feel defeated and of little value. But that is not what we are. We are God's sheep, and He is an encourager. He sacrificed His beloved Son on the cross to give us the victory. Satan is always available to try to convince you otherwise and can be quite convincing at times.

I had just finished several semesters of public speaking in college and was ready to share the message burning in my heart. My daughter Lisa and her band were asked to fill in for someone at a gospel mission men's service, and my husband and I went along to listen. They did a wonderful job musically, but when they finished, no one gave an altar call. It drove me crazy. All those men were there, penniless, homeless, hurting, and entertained, but they weren't given an opportunity to meet the One who could help them the most.

I asked the man in charge if there might be a possibility that I could share a message with them sometime. He recommended going to the women's mission. When I persisted, he told me to ask my pastor and to go through him. The next day I called him and was referred to his assistant, Pastor John, who was out for a week. On finally hearing from him, I learned he did have a program going there and actually needed someone to speak on Monday nights. Then his voice dropped and hinted of concern. "But generally we have men that serve that position."

I was determined I could do it and finally talked him into giving me a try. The first opportunity would be a month away during the week of Thanksgiving. I was excited. I had never had a real audience before, and I wanted so badly to reach those poor men for the Lord. I gathered material and studied. Ideas swam in my head.

Finally I was prepared and well rehearsed. A few days before I was to go, I again called Pastor John for prayer. "Oh," he said, "I forgot all about you and arranged a young man to go that night."

I was stunned. "But I have worked very hard on my sermon. Couldn't you call the young man and tell him your error?" I pleaded.

He reluctantly agreed to do it.

After our conversation, I didn't feel good about myself. Was I being pushy? Was I out of God's will? Perhaps I was forcing a door open that really I was not to walk through. But it was done, and I had to go now.

I took my daughter with me to lead worship, and my husband worked the overhead projector. Lisa and I generally prayed together before we started ministering, so we went into the kitchen area and closed the door. Immediately one of the men who was mentally ill jumped to his feet and began banging on the door, screaming at us. We looked heavenward. After someone helped pull him from the door, we emerged a little shaken but hopefully not showing it. Lisa tried to get some pretty unenthusiastic men to sing along. They looked weary, spent. Not much response for all her efforts.

I then stood up and gave my well-worked-over message. I read an old English poem about the joy of giving something away when you had very little. It was about an old widow who made a pie and gave it to a fatherless family, who gave a slice to a homeless man, who gave the crumbs to the birds. They seemed to like it. Then I went on to my text and summed it up with an altar call. I confused the whole thing by asking them to come forward if they needed prayer as well, and I didn't know who was coming forward for what.

The first man walked around me, so I thought he was going to take the flag down or something until I felt his presence too near me from behind. I stepped forward. So did he. I stepped forward again. He did too. My eyes searched the crowd rapidly for my husband, who was visiting with someone in the back of the room. I stepped off the stage and took a few steps away when suddenly I realized I was leaving my daughter behind with this pervert. I turned around to hear her telling him off for bothering her mother, and then two men bodily escorted him from the building. What a mess. I was shaken, upset, and extremely afraid I was not in God's will. We left saying little to each other that night.

The following week I tried to figure out how to tell my pastor I had failed and to please replace me. On Saturday I had still done nothing about it but remained in my depressed state. A scripture came to me. I couldn't seem to shake it. It played over and over in my head. The words were from Psalm 3:3, "But you are a shield around me, O Lord; you bestow glory on me and lift up my head." It made me feel a little better, but I was still struggling with the next Monday's sermon bearing down on me.

By Sunday I was in desperate need of encouragement from somebody. Sitting in church and waiting for the service to begin, I saw a man who had been at the gospel mission the week before. I walked over and sat down next to him. "Do you usually come to this church?" I asked.

"No," he replied, "but I missed my bus this morning, so I thought I'd try this one. It is walking distance from the gospel mission where I am staying."

"Tell me," I said, "have you been at the gospel mission very long?"

"Yeah, I've been there several times, but no one gets to stay there longer than a month," he replied.

"Do you have a speaker or music there every night?" I continued.

He nodded. "We don't get to eat or stay there unless we listen to their service."

"Really. What kind of sermons do you hear there? Do you ever hear one that really makes an impact on the men?"

I could see he was deep in thought. "Yeah," he finally replied. "There was a lady and her daughter who came. I think it was last Monday night. Several of the guys gave their lives to Jesus that night."

He hadn't recognized me. God had blinded him to who I was so Jesus could give me an encouraging word through him. And boy, was I encouraged! God knew my heart was not to push someone else out of an opportunity to speak. My heart loved those dear men and wanted them to find hope and love in Jesus. God gave me that desire. Satan had tried everything he could to stop me.

My daughter, husband, and I went back the following Monday and brought some more wonderful men to their Savior. I made sure my husband remained in the front pew, and everyone knew he was there. Everything went smoothly. We served there for a year and a half with never another incident. Jesus was the lifter of my head, and together we brought home His lost sheep. Praise God!

CHAPTER 20

❧

SOME JUST GIVE UP

SHEEP ARE NOTORIOUS for giving up when they get sick. If a temperature goes unchecked, a sheep will quit eating and be dead in a day or two. The shepherd must be on the alert at all times for any sign of illness or trouble with his flock. He often needs to take immediate action to save a sheep's life. Often he must work night and day feeding his sheep with liquid he basically pours down her throat until the fever is down and she will eat again.

Annabelle was my first purebred Hampshire ewe. Though she was not a first-class champion by any means, she was my sheep and I loved her. After giving birth to her second set of lambs, she got mastitis in her udder. When I found her in the morning, she refused to stand up and was unwilling to eat.

For sixteen days I fed her an electrolyte solution with a turkey baster four times per day. I milked infection mixed with blood out of her udder. I gave her shots of penicillin twice a day.

She responded to my love and care, but I could see she wasn't going to make it, which was breaking my heart. On the seventeenth day I couldn't do it anymore. I sent my husband instead. She was dead by afternoon. I believe she hung on so long just for me. When I didn't come that last morning, she gave up.

Sheep are so delicate; they require consistent care. There was nothing more I could do but watch the life ebb out of my precious little girl.

Like sheep, we are very easily discouraged. Many of us give up though our Good Shepherd patiently watches over us and is very much at work in our lives. Discouragement is one of Satan's favorite tools.

I have a very dear friend who has chosen a path other than Jesus. Though I see danger ahead, though I see the anguish of her mother, I cannot seem to bring her to Christ. I had so much success in bringing others to know the Lord that her withdrawal only obsessed me more and more to share with her at every opportunity. A wall of resistance was growing between us. I felt over time we had nothing in common. Nothing I said seemed to make a dent. I, like Jesus, want none to perish. Especially one so close to me.

Then one day my husband accused me, "You are doing more harm than good. You are pushing her away from God."

I was totally crushed. His words were like a boulder dropped upon my already discouraged heart. Didn't he understand that time was short? I knew there was a key to unlock her blindness. I was just trying to find it. Didn't he know I would never intentionally hurt anyone?

After the initial shock of his statement, I began to suspect he was right. I was devastated by the thought that I could be responsible for turning someone away from God.

The hurt was so overwhelming that I could no longer minister. I tried for a little while, but I could not hear from God. I was trying to paddle my own boat, and I was failing miserably.

Finally, I quit going to the gospel mission and the youth detention center where God had used me to bring many into His loving arms. I withdrew into my own little corner and anguished over it for months. Although it is very hard to take criticism from a loved one, I'm sure he was right to some extent. I just wished he could tell me those things without making me feel like such a bad person. Didn't he know my heart, after all these years?

I guess I hurt the most because I felt he didn't really accept me for who I was. He didn't understand that I was doing my best.

Then one day the Lord spoke to my mind.

"It is not you I am working on through this, but your husband."

My husband had hurt me before with words, demeaning me to a point of feeling worthless and driving me to near suicide before we were Christians. Words can devastate, especially when erupting from a parent or spouse. I have seen many suffer with much more verbal abuse in their homes than I had ever had to endure. I sometimes wonder how they can ever hold their heads up at all. Verbal abuse is extremely hard to live with. It is as if Satan is living in your house, following you around, focusing on you, pressuring you, squashing you under his thumb.

It is sad so many of us spend our energy accusing others, tearing them down instead of building them up. The result is everyone is unhappy except, of course, Satan. He is delighted that we are falling right into his plan.

I had nearly forgotten those days before we were Christians. I had since felt such a change in our lives had taken place. I had found new value in knowing my Savior had given His life for me, and my husband had been much more loving and kind too. This was like a terrible flashback that I never wanted to feel again.

Then the Lord showed me a vision. I saw a beautiful sailboat on a bright sunny day. The wind was blowing full into her sails, and the water splashed white and sparkling at her bow. "This is you," He said, "when I am blowing upon you with My Spirit. You are strong and willing to go wherever I send you. But you must wait for My wind to power you. Now, look at this picture."

He then showed me a vision of the same beautiful sailboat, except this time it sat in calm, turquoise-colored water. The anchor out, but still just a gentle breeze in its sails. "This is you also," said the Lord. "Be at peace and rest while I do a work in your husband's heart. I have not left you."

My husband had watched how devastated I was. He had been accompanying me to the mission and the youth center and had seen the work God was doing through me suddenly stop. He could see how his words had affected me, and learned to be more tender and loving in the future. God did a wonderful work in both our hearts and in our marriage that year. When at last I could rest until God was again ready to use me, I was free to spend time with my husband and our love grew deeper than ever before.

Finally God's call came to me to go to an all-night intercessory prayer vigil with one hundred ladies before the first March for Jesus event in Seattle. I contemplated in my mind, *But God, I haven't even been reading my Bible. How can I get back into things this quickly?*

His answer was simple and perfect. *"Jump."*

Even though I had given up and literally died to ministering, God, the Good Shepherd, had not given up on me or my husband. He had plans for us, and we both needed a little sandpapering. Though I could not see why God was allowing me to go through that awful hurt one more time, now I see the treasure in it. Rejoice in all things? That's a hard one, but the more I look back at God's work in my life, the more I am able to do just that and look forward to the treasure in the end result.

My husband has been attending Promise Keepers now for several years. He calls me "the best" now, and I'm beginning to believe it.

CHAPTER 21

A HEART FOR THE LOST

HAVE YOU EVER PRAYED one of those prayers that you forgot you had prayed, and then when you realized what was going on, you wish you hadn't?

I was preparing to give an evangelical meeting for up to three hundred people. Everything was set in motion. I had arranged the advertising for a Halloween mime show. The location had been approved and secured. The insurance was taken care of, and performers were practicing their acts. The music, chairs, and microphones had been arranged. The only thing left to take care of was my heart.

The feelings just weren't there. I couldn't seem to communicate with God, but I was going to a retreat two weeks before the event. Surely He would put some feelings back into me. It was probably too many business arrangements to take care of, but what I really needed was a heart for the lost. I was to be the evangelist to call people to salvation.

The first day of the retreat, I made a decision to write down my prayer request and submit it. "Lord Jesus, give me Your heart for the lost." Then I forgot about it, sat back, and enjoyed the retreat.

The month before, I had been to a fair with six of my sheep. They seemed fine when I left for the retreat, but on returning home just three days later I noticed one had a film over her eyes and was walking blindly into walls. I began checking others and found fifteen of my forty-plus sheep had pink eye.

Pink eye in sheep is sometimes very destructive. If left untreated, it can cause severe damage to the eye and even blindness. I headed for the vet, who gave me a medicine to put in their eyes twice a day. He advised me to give them a shot every three days of LA 200, which is an antibiotic and is extremely painful to them when injected. He also warned me that cleanliness was extremely important because the antibiotic could cause abscesses if not done just right. He then told me to keep fly spray on their faces because flies carry the disease from one sheep to another.

I rushed home and separated the flock, putting the unaffected as far away from the infected as possible. Then I started catching them one by one. I put a squirt of ointment in each eye as they struggled mightily with me, wiped their faces with fly ointment, and lastly gave them their shot. The shot was so painful that some quit eating and just stood in a corner with their backs hunched, trying to endure the pain.

After several days of this, obviously they wanted nothing to do with me and ran at the sight of me. Administering this treatment was a painful workout for me as well. Not only did it grieve me to watch them cringe in pain after their shot, but to see seven of them go blind just about broke my heart.

It is not easy to hold a 300-pound animal still when it's afraid of you. I wound up with quite a few aching muscles and bruises as well as sore feet from being stepped on. But every time I tried to back off, they got worse. Not only that, but the others I had separated all had it now too. I was treating eighty eyes, twice a day, for three and a half months before the fly season was over and the disease finally subsided.

I had prayed and cast Satan out. I had anointed them with oil and asked friends and the church to pray. I tried several different kinds of pink-eye remedies. Yet the disease continued, and my heart ached for them. At the end, I was able to bring six of the seven back from blindness, but one lamb, Delightful, could not be helped. She remained blind in one eye.

After the turmoil was over, I had time to contemplate what had gone on. My dear Lord had shown me His heart for those who remain in darkness. He showed me how He constantly battles the enemy who wants to keep us blind. He showed me how He is wounded personally in the battle for us. How we fight Him when He is trying to help us. He showed me how His heart aches for those who backslide once they have seen the light. He showed me that sometimes He has to allow hurt in our lives to bring us out of blindness. He showed me how He doesn't give up, how He tries everything He can to save us. I had battled blindness in my lambs for only three and one-half months. He had battled for my sight for thirty-five years.

CHAPTER 22

TEMPTATION

SHEEP ARE NOTORIOUS for getting out of their fences. I'm sure whoever coined the phrase "The grass is greener on the other side of the fence" owned sheep.

Our first fence was made out of chicken wire because we had chickens before our daughter was blessed with receiving her first two ewes. The sheep crawled under it. Our second fence was welded wire. They climbed it and bent it to the ground.

Finally we got New Zealand hot wire—seven strands of very thick, very electric wire. That did the trick. Our neighbors, who had purchased some of our sheep and had some lambs of their own, had very thin, very loose hot wire that had kept their horse and cattle in just fine. But the sheep thought nothing of charging through it to get into the next yard, where the people had meticulously taken care of their lovely green lawn. Soon they were New Zealand fence owners too.

Driving by one day I was noticing how content their sheep looked grazing in the middle of their field. There were no more attempts at escape because the boundary lines had been firmly set. I could see how this applies also to raising children. They need firm boundaries too. Inconsistency in parenting is like having no fence at all, and children who wander without guidelines suffer.

I often thought God was awfully harsh in some of His punishments in the Old Testament. But I noticed also how a second chance was always given. In Genesis, Cain brought his offering of fruit and vegetables to the altar as a sacrifice to God because he was a farmer and he was proud of his crops. His brother Abel brought his lamb. God did not accept Cain's offering because a blood offering was necessary to remedy sin. God was giving us an example of the sacrifice of Jesus, the Lamb of God, who would take away the sin of the world.

When Cain showed his anger at not being appreciated for his efforts, God said, "Do what is right, and will you not be accepted?"

Right there God showed that even though we sin, the blood of the lamb to come would give us the second chance. He would provide an opportunity to be born again, forgiven, and put on the right path. But sadly, Cain passed up the opportunity God gave him. His pride caused him to sin, and jealousy consumed him to the point of murdering his brother. He was cast out away from his family and lived the rest of his life separated from them and from God.

The boundaries are there, the line is drawn, but God calls us to choose life. He has made a way for us to follow and left instructions by way of the Bible. Jesus said to the woman caught in the act of adultery, "Go now and sin no more." He would not say to us, "Sin no more," if we were unable to stop sinning.

We never know however when temptation is going to come knocking at our door. It doesn't matter how long you have been saved or what position you hold in life. Satan never stops trying to bring you down.

We discovered that quite a few people lie about the age of their sheep in competitions. We try to get them born in December or January, which is about the earliest possible because of the ewe's breeding cycle. When the judge at the fair looks at the sheep, all supposedly the same age, he will naturally lean to a lamb that is bigger because it will produce more meat or wool faster than the others. This is all fine and good except some of the competitors show a December-born lamb as a February lamb. Of course, the lamb towers above the others and often wins first place.

The competition can get pretty tough with the prize money and worth of your sheep going up with each win, especially in national competition. We have seen some of our breed of sheep sell for as much as $9,000.

One day temptation came knocking at our door. We had two lambs born on December 30. They would be small for the December class, but big for the January class. It would be so easy to register them as January lambs. After all, who would know? Everybody else does it, don't they? (Two of Satan's favorite arguments.) Somehow we overcame the temptation. Lo and behold, everyone else had small December lambs that year, so no one brought them but us. We took first place at every fair we went to that year! God is so good to reward us when we overcome the enemy with righteousness.

When I was a little girl, I used to watch Charlton Heston in *The Ten Commandments*. Even though I did not know God yet, I believed we were supposed to keep those commandments. Yet one day I slipped.

My husband and I were young and struggling financially. We each had a job and were trying to get ahead. We had bought a rundown, condemned house and were working on it every evening. We needed to buy some lumber and noticed an ad in the paper. A man had shut down his lumberyard and had a garage full of lumber that he said he would sell at below cost. At the time, we had an old '52

Chevy pickup with running boards on it. We filled it with what we needed and paid the man $250, a lot more than we thought it would be.

We were ready to leave when I noticed a pile of 1x1s. I asked the man if I could have a couple to stake up my tomato plants.

"They are one dollar each," he cold heartily replied.

I had no cash on me and didn't want to write a check for two dollars. I felt he could have given them to us for all we had purchased from him. (Satan always helps you justify your sin.) When he went back in his house and we had tied our red flag on the back, I threw a couple of stakes in and off we went.

Halfway home our red flag blew off. I got out of the truck to run back for it, but the wind was blowing so hard I couldn't catch up with it. My husband backed up the truck and suggested I stand on the running board and hang on, and he would drive me back to get it. He was going about thirty-five miles per hour when suddenly I couldn't hang on anymore. I fell on the pavement on my knees. I knew they were both shattered.

Right then the only thought in my mind was I had broken God's commandment, "Thou shall not steal." I told God right then and there, "If You will make my knees be all right, I will take the stakes back and I will never steal again."

Miraculously, I got up without a bruise or a scratch, and we took the stakes right back to where they belonged.

When sheep get out of their pasture, they subject themselves to attacks by dogs or coyotes. They may even get hit by a car. By breaking God's law's, we subject ourselves to whatever Satan wants to throw at us. God's laws are to keep us safe. Just think if everyone were to obey His commandments. We would need no police or jails or lawyers. No one would live in fear of another. That is what God wants. Isn't it what we want too?

CHAPTER 23

WHO IS MY SHEPHERD?

MY SHEEP KNOW ME, just as I know them. I amazed myself once with just how familiar they are to me. While looking for one particular sheep, I approached a group from behind as they were eating out of their feeders. I discovered that I knew them not only by their faces but by the texture and crimp of their wool, by their shape, and even by the way their udders hung. I love to amaze people by calling my sheep from the gate. They can be out of sight, several hundred feet away, but when they hear me call, "Come on," they appear from all directions, jump with joy, and come running to where I am.

They never cease to amaze and amuse me. During one of those nativity scene dramas they participated in each Christmas, my husband tied Angelica on a rope that was a little too long. As Mary laid baby Jesus in the trough, Angelica went to have a look. Another two inches and she would have probably tried to have a bite, but it seemed as if she was looking adoringly at the new Christ child along

141

with Joseph and Mary. She had the audience fooled, but I knew what she was thinking!

At home the sheep are perfectly comfortable being around my husband and me; but let a stranger walk into an area where they are eating, and they will scatter. I often just stand and watch them as they eat or nurse their young. They are at ease in my presence unless, of course, I have a shot needle in my hand!

Someone asked me an interesting question that started me on some deep thinking. She asked, "Who is the Bride, and who are the guests at the wedding banquet?"

We had been studying the Song of Solomon. I reflected back to a verse I had just read.

> Friends: How is your beloved better than others, most beautiful of women? How is your beloved better than others, that you charge us so?
>
> Beloved: My lover is radiant and ruddy, outstanding among ten thousand. His head is purest gold; his hair is wavy and black as a raven. His eyes are like doves by the water streams, washed in milk, mounted like jewels. His cheeks are like beds of spice yielding perfume. His lips are like lilies dripping with myrrh. His arms are rods of gold set with chrysolite. His body is like polished ivory decorated with sapphires. His legs are pillars of marble set on bases of pure gold. His appearance is like Lebanon, choice as its cedars. His mouth is sweetness itself; he is altogether lovely. This is my lover, this my friend, O daughters of Jerusalem. (Song of Sol. 5:9–16)

She knows her shepherd or beloved from head to foot. You can tell by her description of him that she is deeply in love. But there is more to this story.

Her friends ask, "Where has your lover gone, most beautiful of women? Which way did your lover turn, that we may look for him with you?" (Song of Sol. 6:1).

She responds, "My lover has gone down to his garden, to the beds of spices, to browse in the gardens and to gather lilies. I am my lover's and my lover is mine; he browses among the lilies" (vv. 2–3).

Not only can she tell them what he looks like in great detail, but she also knows where he is and what he is doing.

See this in contrast to the man in the parable of the talents (see Matt. 25:14–30). A master is about to go away, and he divides his money between his three servants to invest while he is gone. The first two invested their money and had a profit for their master upon his return. They were commended for their goodness and faithfulness.

The last hid his talent in the ground and upon his master's return admitted in verse 24, "Master, I knew that you are a hard man, harvesting where you have not sown and gathering where you have not scattered seed. So I was afraid and went out and hid your talent in the ground. See, here is what belongs to you."

He did not know his master at all. He allowed fear to limit him. He did not bless and speak of his master in love, but feared him. But the same master was master of all three.

The Pharisees were the spiritual leaders of the Jewish people in the days of Jesus. They read the Torah and even lived in the temple. Yet when Jesus came, they did not recognize Him. They didn't understand Him. They did not *know* Him.

As I was looking through my Bible one day for a certain parable, I noticed a repeated pattern of words in three different parables. Matthew 7:21–23 says, "Not everyone who says to me, 'Lord, Lord' will enter the kingdom of heaven, but only he who does the will of my Father who is in heaven. Many will say to me on that day, 'Lord, Lord, did we not prophesy in your name, and in your name drive out demons and perform many miracles?' Then I will tell them plainly, 'I never knew you. Away from me, you evildoers!'"

This was always a very difficult passage for me to grasp. How could He not know those who called Him Lord? I called Him Lord, and I was involved in doing miracles in

His name. Was there a chance I would not enter the kingdom of heaven?

Then I saw it again. In Matthew 25:1–13, we see the same statement made to five of the ten virgins.

> At that time the kingdom of heaven will be like ten virgins who took their lamps and went out to meet the bridegroom. Five of them were foolish and five were wise. The foolish ones took their lamps but did not take any oil with them. The wise, however, took oil in jars along with their lamps. The bridegroom was a long time in coming, and they all became drowsy and fell asleep.
>
> At midnight the cry rang out: "Here is the bridegroom! Come out to meet him!"
>
> Then all the virgins woke up and trimmed their lamps. The foolish ones said to the wise, "Give us some of your oil; our lamps are going out."
>
> "No," they replied, "there may not be enough for both us and you. Instead, go to those who sell oil and buy some for yourselves."
>
> But while they were on their way to buy the oil, the bridegroom arrived. The virgins who were ready went in with him to the wedding banquet. And the door was shut.
>
> Later the others also came. "Sir! Sir!" they said. "Open the door for us!"
>
> But he replied, "I tell you the truth, I don't know you."
>
> Therefore keep watch, because you do not know the day or the hour.

But Lord, I thought to myself, *they had kept themselves virgins for You, and they were awaiting Your return with the others.* How could the merciful God I had always known shut the door on these women?

As I read the parable of the narrow door in Luke 13:24–28, my understanding was opened.

> Make every effort to enter through the narrow door, because many, I tell you, will try to enter and will not be

able to. Once the owner of the house gets up and closes the door, you will stand outside knocking and pleading, "Sir, open the door for us." But he will answer, "I don't know you or where you come from." Then you will say, "We ate and drank with you, and you taught in our streets." But he will reply, "I don't know you or where you come from. Away from me, all you evildoers!"

Why did He not recognize them if they were on the narrow road?

I have done some speaking, and although many in my audience think they know me because I am open and share my life stories, I do not know them unless they come up, introduce themselves, and share their lives with me. Even though those people had eaten with and listened to the Master, they apparently did not make an attempt at a personal relationship with Him.

The five virgins who were short of oil for their lamps were followers of people, not of God. They were taking directions from the other virgins, who apparently had been in communication with God and knew what was needed at the right moment. They did not ask their lover; they asked other people what to do. There was no one-on-one relationship with the bridegroom.

The people who did miracles in Jesus' name did them because the name of Jesus is powerful. They called Him Lord but apparently did not know Him as Lord. When you know Him as Lord, you will recognize that only He heals and touches hearts. You want only Him to receive the glory for what He has done through you. The Bible says God can even use a donkey to speak through if He so chooses.

When you know your shepherd as the Good Shepherd, you will find Him trustworthy. You will know He has good things in store for you. As you know Him as provider, you will not be worried about your money, like the man in the parable of the talents was. As you know Him as your Bridegroom, you will be in love with Him and be eagerly listening for His every whisper. As you know Him as your Shepherd, you will be willing to go through any gate He opens for you.

Many of us hesitate at a new opportunity God opens up for us. Some miss the adventure of a lifetime because of fear of leaving our old pasture or comfort zone. We place more trust in the old pasture than we do in our Shepherd. Sit down like Mary at His feet. Get to know the One who desires to make you His bride. Spend time with Him. Ask Him questions, then listen for His answers. Tell Him your sad times and share with Him your joys.

Relationship is the answer. Jeremiah 29:11 says, "'For I know the plans I have for you,' declares the Lord, 'plans to prosper you and not to harm you, plans to give you hope and a future.'"

We are not saved just to go to heaven, but to have an incredible walk with our Lord here on earth. Learning and trusting and growing more each day, and occasionally participating in one of His fantastic miracles, we can have the life God intends us to have.

I once had a small, short-legged ewe I bred to a ram with long legs. When she gave birth, both her lambs resembled the long-legged father. She was a good mother with lots of milk, but her udder nearly touched the ground because of her short legs. When I found our new set of twins, they were searching desperately to find their source of milk in all the wrong places.

I knelt down on the ground and took the little girl lamb, putting her over one of my legs. I bent her front knees, held her chin in one hand and the ewe's teat in the other, and gave her a taste of warm milk. I had to do this three times before she finally realized she would have to get down low to get any milk. When I was satisfied that she knew what she was doing, I went around to the other side of the very patient mother and picked up her new son. Straddling him over my leg, I endeavored to bend his knees to get down to where we needed to be. But every time I let go of his legs, he stubbornly straightened them right back up again. Having only two hands to work with, I grew quite frustrated. I finally tried holding him sideways so I could squirt some milk in his mouth, but his lips were sealed. I could not get him to nurse.

After struggling with him for about a half an hour, I decided to let him go for a while. *He'll get good and hungry, and then I'll be able to work with him,* I hoped. One hour later, at 4:00 A.M., I was back in the barn. Both lambs were sleeping, looking quite content. But I wasn't, because I could not tell if he had eaten or not. So down we went again but with the same results. His little will said, "No! I won't bend my knees," and, "No! I won't open my mouth no matter how hard you try to make me."

All through the day I tried and tried. Finally I concluded that he must be getting some when I was not looking. He seemed content and wasn't crying. Later that night I went out again to find our little guy dead.

No shepherd likes to lose a lamb. He looked flat, and at first I thought perhaps his mother had laid on him. I went into the house asking God why.

I opened my Bible to Lamentations 4:9 and read, "It is better to die by the sword, than to starve."

"But God," I plead, "I tried so hard. Why did he die?"

God spoke to my mind, "I wanted to show you something. Your lamb had a good shepherd, who tried very hard to give him the source of life, out of love and knowledge. He had a mother who was patient with him. He was in a place of safety in your barn. He had a sister whom he could see and hear receiving the source of life, yet he would not bend his knee. It is the same with My sheep. I have sheep that go into the safety of My church. They have a good shepherd telling them about the source of life and how to receive Me. They see others going to the altar, surrendering their pride and receiving the source of life. Yet they will not bend their knee and repent of their ways. They will not open their mouths and confess Me as their Savior and Lord. My heart aches for them just as your heart hurts for your lamb."

So many people go through the motions of going to church and hearing the message, but they do not surrender their lives to God. They go on only to find in the end the door will be shut to them because they do not know their Shepherd, and He does not know them.

If this is you, Jesus is waiting with His arms outstretched to you, but He has given you the choice. He knows where you are headed; so do you. Ask Him to forgive your sins. Get down on your knees if you like, but the words from your heart are enough. Ask Him to be your Lord and Savior right now. He will. Then tell somebody. The joy will flood into you as the burdens come off.

You have already gotten to know Him some as you have been reading this book. You will get to know Him even more as you read your Bible and go to church. The more time you spend getting to know Him, the faster you will grow spiritually. You will discover that He can and will speak to you as you ask Him questions. Sometimes a scripture will seemingly stand out to you as you are reading. Sometimes the pastor will preach on just what you needed to know. Sometimes you will hear Him in your mind. It is incredible to think we can know the King of kings, and the Lord of lords, the Good Shepherd.

In John 20, Jesus told His disciples to "receive the Holy Spirit." You need only to ask Jesus to fill you with the Holy Spirit, and He will. The Holy Spirit is the third person of God. He came down from heaven shortly after Jesus ascended. Jesus did not leave us alone, but sent the Teacher, the Counselor, to help us grow and overcome the enemy's hold on us.

You will soon find He is your best friend and constant companion. He nudges me into prayer for my children. He gives us words of knowledge. He will teach us all we need to know and give us the boldness to proclaim God's message.

Ask now, and then study the Books of John, Acts, and 1 Corinthians for a deeper understanding of the wonder that just took place in your life.

CHAPTER 24

୨ଈ

FEED MY SHEEP

WHILE VISITING ISRAEL, we learned something of Jewish custom. Whenever there is a disagreement to be settled, one man will fix a meal for the other. If the other man joins him, he is willing to discuss the matter.

After the resurrection, Jesus Christ appeared to His disciples who had returned to the lifestyle they had chosen before they had met their Lord. They were fishing. On shore, Jesus was preparing some breakfast for them. Apparently He had something important He wanted to get settled.

After hearing Jesus call out to them, they recognized the Lord for who He was. Peter could not wait to see Him and jumped into the water and swam ashore.

"Come have some breakfast," Jesus invited.

When they had finished eating, Jesus said to Simon Peter, "Simon son of John, do you truly love me more than these?"

"Yes, Lord," he said, "you know that I love you."

Jesus said, "Feed my lambs."

Again Jesus said, "Simon son of John, do you truly love me?"

He answered again, "Yes Lord, you know that I love you."

Jesus said, "Take care of my sheep."

The third time he said to him, "Simon son of John, do you love me?"

Peter was hurt because Jesus asked him the third time, "Do you love me?" He said, "Lord, you know all things; you know that I love you."

Jesus said, "Feed my sheep." (John 21:15–17)

I had always understood the purpose of this passage was to restore Peter to grace. He had suffered with his human weakness when he denied knowing Jesus just before the crucifixion. He had denied the Lord three times, and three times he was asked, "Do you love Me?" Yet standing on the shores of Lake Tiberias, where this all happened, and reflecting on what had just taken place before we had left for Israel, I discovered a much deeper meaning.

We had a three-year-old ewe named Angelica that had not gotten pregnant when she had been bred by the ram. We waited the five months of gestation, but when nothing happened, we put her back in with the ram. She didn't need any special diet until the last six weeks of her pregnancy, so I left her out in the pasture with the ewes that were weaning their lambs.

In all the hustle and bustle of moving sheep from one pasture to the next and lambs being born, she slipped my mind. I normally would have moved her into the barn area, where I could have watched her more closely and fed her better as she neared her time to lamb. As a result she came down with pregnancy toxemia. Two weeks before her due date, she quit eating and drinking and lay down to die.

When I realized my mistake, I felt terrible. I called the vet, who told me that I should bring her in for a cesarean section to get the lambs out or I might lose her. When I questioned him about the lambs survival rate this early, he didn't give me any hope. Their respiratory system would not be fully developed, and they would probably die. It would be difficult, but I didn't want to lose any of them, so I decided against operating. I determined to keep her alive, no matter what I had to do, until her due date. Hopefully her lambs would make it too. Once she gave birth, the toxemia would subside.

We began by giving her electrolytes and Karo syrup mixed with water, squirting it into her mouth with a turkey baster. I went out to the barn as frequently as possible, each time taking a quart of the mixture with me. I held her head in my lap, being careful that she would not choke and get it into her lungs. Each time I got the sticky liquid all over her and me, but most of it went down. I then stuffed some grain in her mouth by hand. After spitting most of it out, she chewed maybe a teaspoon of it at a time. The only time she got up was overnight when I left some alfalfa in front of her. I went back early in the morning to see her facing the opposite direction. The sight of food must have been repulsive to her. Yet, on we struggled.

Sheep normally start eating as soon as the sun comes up and continue until it is dark out. She wasn't getting much to sustain her and her lambs, but she still raised her head and perked up her ears when she heard me coming.

On the twelfth day, there was no sign she was nearing labor or any milk was coming in. She had been through enough, and at this stage I felt I could possibly save the lambs if they were still alive. I had seen no movement, yet she had not aborted them either. I called the vet. He gave me the go ahead to give her a shot to induce labor.

"You will have to watch her every hour for up to twenty-four hours," he warned me. "If she is this weak, she may not be able to deliver them and may die trying."

I was exhausted to begin with, but I had not come this far to let her die now. My dear husband and I took turns going out every hour until finally, after twenty hours, her water broke. After waiting and seeing no attempt at contractions, I reached in to see if I could feel any feet. She was fully dilated, yet there was no lamb near the birth canal. I reached in farther until up to my elbow, and I found one. He pulled his foot back when I tried to get a hold of it.

"I've got one," I gratefully shouted to my husband who was holding the mother's head, "and it's alive!"

It was not easy. The lamb's head was turned back and was stuck. I worked with one hand for nearly an hour to get him in the right position to be pulled out. Much to our relief, he was born alive and adorable. Fifteen pounds and looking very much like a little ram, complete with bulging muscles in his bowed legs.

For the ewe to be that ill, it had to be a multiple birth. I reached in again and pulled a sixteen-pound, very feminine ewe lamb from the mother's womb. Suddenly, to our amazement, the mother rose up and began caring for and licking her new lambs. Her intentions were fully there, but she tired quickly. We had to take over the drying process.

The lambs were very weak. We rubbed them briskly to try to stimulate blood circulation, but it was obvious they were not going to be able to nurse or stand up by themselves. The mother was unable to stand and nurse them. We took them into the house and laid them on newspapers and towels in front of our wood stove, where we tube fed them for the first four days. We wrapped them up in towels to keep them warm and took them out to the barn every few hours so mama would not forget them. I tried to stimulate her udder to produce some colostrum for them. Though there was very little, it was enough mixed with formula to get them started in life.

It is very touch and go with lambs at this stage. I had lost several that were not nearly as weak as these. Now we had three sick sheep to care for instead of just one. On the second day the little girl, Missy, wobbled to her feet. Finally, on the fifth day and after much coaxing, she took a bottle. The mother too was starting to eat on her own. We were gaining on the situation, but the little boy had been much weaker. It took a few more days to see results in him. By then I had trained Missy to nurse from her mother, although mama still had very little milk. But our little boy, now named Luke, wanted nothing to do with that big fuzzy animal in the barn. He was convinced I was his mother. We had to feed them both by bottle every three hours, day and night.

I have found that a shepherd's life is not easy. As I pondered God's heart in the matter, I could see the parallel. God's heart is that none should perish. He also showed me that when there is a flickering wick of life that cannot quite make it to the altar, He reaches down into the depths of darkness and meets us there.

This passage reminded me of what we had just experienced.

> He reached down from on high and took hold of me; He drew me out of deep waters, He rescued me from my powerful enemy, from my foes, who were too strong for me. They confronted me in the day of my disaster but the Lord was my support. He brought me out into a spacious place; He rescued me because he delighted in me. (2 Sam. 22:17–21)

Many afternoons as Angelica was recovering I would put a halter on her and walk out in the pasture with her lambs following close behind. I lay down in the green pasture while she enjoyed the fresh grass to eat, and the lambs frolicked playfully around us. Luke got too warm and lay down next to me in my shade. I loved watching them. I loved being needed, but I knew it would be better for him if he would realize who his real mother was.

Jesus is also concerned about our relationships. Even if our mother or father is unable to be there for us when we are young, God is watching over us. As He is working to get us on our feet, He is also ministering to our parents. His goal is that we are all healed and able to be together as a loving family.

As days went by we were happy to see all doing well and gaining weight. I was able to feed them more milk less often now that they were two weeks old. I knew, however, that we would soon be leaving for Israel. Stress built as I realized that the mother was not getting enough milk in to feed her two lambs. All my attempts at getting little Luke to eat from his mother were in vain. Who could I possibly ask to take over such a task as feeding my lambs every four hours? I started calling friends, first with Stephanie and Brenda next door, who normally took care of my sheep when I was away.

"I just started a job at Boeing, and they are working me sixteen hours a day," Stephanie apologized, "but Brenda could probably feed them in the evening after school."

I called my daughter Lisa.

"Well, Mom, I guess I could feed them at 2:30 every day."

I called my other daughter, Rebecca.

"Can't you find someone closer?"

I called another neighbor. She didn't call back.

I called a friend who had sheep.

"I'm going to be out of town at the same time you are," she said, "otherwise, I'd be happy to help."

I put an ad in the paper, trying to find someone who would take some bottle babies. I got one call, but he didn't show up on the day he said he would come. I desperately called him back and let him know my situation. He again said he would come and get them but mentioned he hadn't realized he would have to feed them all night as well. He said he wouldn't be able to come until the day after I was to leave, so I had to make arrangements for Rebecca to keep them at her house until he got there. I didn't know if he would follow through on his commitment or if he was having second thoughts because of the night feedings. So I continued my quest to find backup help.

Another potential problem was taking both lambs away from the mother so suddenly. Now that she was getting milk in, she might develop mastitis in her udder and die from that. I decided to leave Missy with her and hope the two supplement feedings would see her through.

Two days before we were to leave, we were over at my daughter Lisa's house for Mother's Day. I wanted to confirm that she would be there to feed her at 2:30 as she had agreed.

"Oh," she suddenly realized, "I can't do it on Sundays. That's church, and afterwards we always spend it with Rich's parents in Redmond."

It was too much. I burst out in tears. I couldn't stand the thought of my two little babies, which had been through so much and come so far, abandoned at this point in life. But I could find no one I could depend on to help me.

Seeing my distress, Lisa offered to ask a friend of hers who had sheep if she would take them while I was gone.

Much to my relief she said she would, although when I called her to let her know how grateful I was, she sounded very put out.

"I didn't offer to do this. I was asked to. You know you are asking a lot. We had plans too, and Lisa is going to have to come out here and spend some time. It is not convenient for any of us, you know, and this is going to cost you."

Feeling absolutely miserable, I thanked her anyway and took little Luke to Rebecca's house. She had set out an expandable wooden pen in her backyard for him. I reluctantly sat him down for the last time. He cried out to me and jumped at the fence separating us over and over. My heart was breaking as I walked away and left for Israel, not knowing what was going to become of my precious lambs.

Standing a few days later on the shore where Jesus had reappeared to His disciples, I heard the words of our Lord in a different way. I could picture Him looking deep into Peter's eyes as He asked him three times: "Peter, do you love Me? Feed My sheep."

It was a desperate cry from a Shepherd who loved His sheep. My mind flashed back to my lambs left at home and how brokenhearted I had been at the response of my plea for help. Jesus also had to go away and leave his new lambs in the hands of others. Would they be loved as He had loved them? Would they be fed when they needed feeding, or would inconvenience cause them to go hungry? Would those He had trained and trusted understand the importance of their calling? Would they go back to fishing or would they pick up their cross and follow Him?

Generations have passed, and faithful followers have heard His cry. Now His lambs are entrusted to us. Will you feed His sheep?

God is good. I returned to find little Luke had a good home with the man who picked him up later that day, and Angelica and Missy were doing fine at home. God is concerned with all that we are concerned with. How wonderful to have the chance to do something for Him.

CHAPTER 25

IT'S TIME

SHEEP ARE BIG ON ROUTINE. Just forget what time it is, or decide to sleep in, and they will let you know loud and clear. "It's feeding time." They are up early in the spring and summer months, then have a time to relax and digest in the middle of the day. Then out they go again toward evening to get their dinner. In winter, we hear lots of commotion coming from the barn if we are late with their breakfast. They stand at their feeders wondering what is wrong with us that we could be so careless about our chores. But do we know what time it is on God's calendar? God says in His Word that He will give us signs so we will know.

We have recently been experiencing a strange happening among various congregations. Laughter and talk of a roar from the Lion of Judah have echoed from followers. Caution and curiosity filled my emotions, but having not experienced anything unusual myself, I simply filed it away as a wait-and-see phenomenon.

Then one day my prodigal son came home, repentant and wanting his life with Jesus back again. Upon sharing this wonderful news with others, I found they too were experiencing the same thing. The prodigals were returning. One had been in the gay lifestyle for years; another had several children all by different men and then turned lesbian. Still another had been in a coma but woke up long enough to accept Christ and then slipped away again.

As we drove to church one morning, I opened my Bible to Hosea 11. It spoke of God's child, Israel, who had been nurtured and loved by Him.

> It was I who taught Ephraim to walk, taking them by the arms; but they did not realize it was I who healed them. I led them with cords of human kindness, with ties of love; I lifted the yoke from their neck and bent down to feed them. (Hosea 11:3–5)

The passage spoke of how they had left Him in a spirit of rebellion, refusing to repent, and how He had grieved for them. Then the most interesting words jumped off the page to me. Verses 10 and 11 say, "They will follow the Lord; he will roar like a lion. When he roars, his children will come trembling from the west. They will come trembling like birds from Egypt, like doves from Assyria. I will settle them in their homes," declares the Lord.

Suddenly the thought struck me that the roar of the lion people were speaking of was a prophetic message from God that the prodigals were coming back to Him. Just as the remnant of Israel was returning to their land and their God, the hard ones to reach, the backsliders, were also on their way home.

As I mentioned earlier, several years ago I brought eight new sheep home and tried to mix them with my flock. The next morning I saw the eight sheep over here and the rest of the flock over there. Day after day they remained separate, until one day we had them all sheared. They all became one flock. As I sat thinking about how God's people are divided over so many issues, I asked God, "How are You going to shear us?" Perhaps He is.

We, like sheep, are a stubborn group. Often we will not change until pressure is exerted. Although God is very patient, the time is drawing near to His return. He wants us unified against Satan and his plans, not against each other. With security in finance being shaken globely and the y 2 k problem facing us– many are realzing the need for something more solid to hang on to.

One way God works is to let us have our own way, but as He takes His hand of protection off us, we feel the wrath of the enemy. During an earthquake we had here last year, my sheep were together at my side in an instant. When a disaster happens, no one seems to care who you are or what denomination you belong to. We all tend to pitch in and help. The Oklahoma bombing was a prime example. Disasters are increasing. When Princess Diana died in a terrible automobile accident, millions of people tuned in to attend her Christian funeral on TV. It gathered us together into one flock.

Soon after, Mother Theresa passed away. Hers was the first Christian funeral ever televised from India. Many various religions and countries paid tribute. We were again joined together. Floods, fires, and earthquakes are increasing all over the globe. Many times Christian ministries are first to be there to help. They bring not only food and medical supplies to the hurting, but also a touch from a God who cares.

Many pastors from various denominations are gathering to repent over their attitudes about one another. In major conferences, racial reconciliation is the main topic. Could it be God gathering us together into one flock?

Another interesting thing is going on in Christian circles. Promise Keepers, which started with a mere handful of men, has been growing at incredible rates. Men are filling stadiums, hands upraised to God, learning how to become the fathers and husbands God called them to be. Could this be the fulfillment of Malachi 4:5 and 6?

See, I will send you the prophet Elijah before that great and dreadful day of the Lord comes. He will turn the hearts of the fathers to their children, and the hearts of the children to their fathers; or else I will come and strike the land with a curse.

On our travels recently to Israel, as I hopped off the plane, a song hit my mind. The message in the song "Jehovah Jireh" talks about Israel being set free in the year of Jubilee.

The year of completion for the Jew is seven, deriving from the Book of Genesis, where it took God seven days to complete the creation of our world. The eighth day to them is a day of new beginnings.

It has been forty-nine years since Israel became a nation—seven sevens. The eighth day is the fiftieth year, 1998 the Year of Jubilee, the celebration of forgiveness of debt. There is deep meaning in those holy times set by God. Are we seeing something incredible happen to our family in Israel? More and more Jews are finding their Messiah in Jesus every day.

I recently had a vision from the Lord. I entered a room filled with gifts. One stood out to me. It was about eighteen inches high, about ten inches wide, and about fourteen inches deep. It was wrapped in a beautiful white paper with big glimmering red polka dots all over it. It had a red ribbon and bow that were indescribable. Jesus handed me the gift.

I can't open this. It is too beautiful, I thought to myself. So He reached in and handed me a watch.

"A watch?" I was surprised and yet disappointed. I expected something wonderful out of such a big and beautiful box.

"It's time," was all He said to me.

A few days later I had dinner with a friend. "Did you go to church on Sunday?" I asked, wondering what the sermon might have been that I had missed.

"No," she said. "My watch broke, and I missed it." Then she went on to tell me that she had a very interesting thing happen as a result. She had gone to the store to get a new one, and when the lady handed it to her over the counter, the Lord said to her, "It's time."

She sat at her kitchen table later that day and studied the watch, trying to understand what God was trying to tell her. That's when she noticed a word printed across the face of the watch. She got her magnifying glass to look closer. The word read NOW.

We all know the time is close for the Lord's return. We also know His heart is that none should perish. Perhaps this is the final harvest.

When we move with God, He makes it easy. Those people you have given up on may be ready now.

Chapter 26

What's Stopping Us?

THERE ARE MANY LOST LAMBS out there. Our hearts go out to a dog running down a road obviously lost, but where is our heart for God's lost? The words of Jesus tell us that the two most important commandments are to "Love the Lord with all your heart, soul, and mind, and love your neighbor as yourself." Yet as we go about our day, are we sharing Jesus with the lost? Are we bringing them to church?

I've been to many outreaches filled with Christians, and very few bring an unsaved friend. They come to enjoy the music and hear the message, and then many think afterward, *That would have been good for my neighbor to hear.* True, there has been a terrible resistance to the Lord, and people have been difficult to witness to in the United States, but I believe that time is over. The harvest is ripe. People are being prepared like never before. They are waiting to hear the good news.

Busyness is a real problem in today's world. So much to do and so little time to do it all. That is why the Lord calls us to sell everything, give it to the poor, and go. There is nothing so wonderful as to be totally free to serve the Lord.

166 / WHAT'S STOPPING US?

My husband and I recently heard that call. We built a little apartment in our basement, gave most of our furniture
away, and found good homes for all our sheep except two.
We rented the upstairs to a family with two girls who
adored the sheep. We were at last ready to answer God's call.

When no direction came as to where to go to serve Him,
we chose to go somewhere warm: Hawaii. On the second
day there, we were asked to host a table of congressmen at
a prayer breakfast. The next week, I was asked to speak to
a group of about two hundred at a secular Christmas dinner program for a community center. My message was anything but secular. I walked a beach with twelve women
from a local fellowship, and in one-and-a-half hours
brought five of the twelve people we met to the Lord. We
were in Hawaii for six months with doors opening before us
daily. God kept giving me the same message everywhere I
went. "Go in confidence."

A senior center had arranged to have an Egyptian healer
come and speak to a group of people one Monday afternoon. I "happened to be" in her office when she found out
he would not be coming after all.

"Do you know anyone who could speak on spiritual
healing?" She was upset at such a late cancellation.

"I can," I suggested. That Monday I gave my testimony
to a group of about thirty and told them about laying hands
on the sick. After several had given their lives to Jesus and
I had prayed for many of them individually for healing, one
lady came back to me.

"I was watching as you prayed for other people. You
touched them on their foreheads or their shoulders. But
when I came up, you touched me on the back of my head,"
she said. "Why did you do that?"

I explained that I was unaware of where I had touched
her, but God knew my hands were available to Him. She
told me that she had experienced throbbing in the back of
her head from a brain aneurism, but when I touched her

there, it stopped pulsating. I had never spoken on healing before, but God opened the door so I went through it.

God once gave me a dream that helps me immensely as I reach out with the good news to people who come across my path. I was in a little rowboat, and the ship I had been traveling in was going down. Many people were in the water. As I reached out to one, he resisted me and said, "No, I don't need your help. I can get there by myself." He didn't realize how far it was to shore.

The next man I reached out to resisted as well. "I like swimming," he called back as he headed out to sea, where sharks awaited him.

But the third man I took hold of was grateful. "I was going down for the last time," he gasped. "Thank God you were here."

"Was I wrong to reach out to the others when they were not ready?" I questioned God.

"No, you were not. When that first man gets tired of swimming, he will remember you and your rowboat. The other will see the sharks ahead, and he too will remember your outstretched arm. Let your light shine to all who live in darkness. Do not let their rejection stop you, for it is only temporary. They will remember when the time comes which way to turn."

A man at our church shared with me recently that he had been in a terrible motorcycle accident when he was only twenty-three. He had been in a coma for over four months and then died. In his death he saw Satan only an inch away from him. He turned from him and cried out to Jesus. "No, I want Jesus!" He turned, and Satan was still there. He cried out again with arms uplifted. "No, I want Jesus!"

The Lord said to him, "Then let go of Satan."

It is wonderful to watch him worship his Savior. Though his body is crippled and his speech is slurred, he is grateful with all his heart, and it shows.

"How did you know to turn to Jesus?" I asked him.

"My mother used to take me to a Catholic church when I was young."

The Lord snatched him from the flames at the last minute because he knew where to turn. Someone had made Jesus known to him.

God has given me a precious gift I want to share with you. It has given me more joy and adventure than anything else in my life. It is the gift of evangelism. I have no fear of asking people if they would like to receive Jesus as their Savior. I would like to show you how easy it is, especially now that I can see it is in God's timing. Perhaps now that you can see God's heart for that lost lamb, you will want to aid in his rescue. Hell is a terrible place, and many unsuspecting people are headed there if we do not share the good news.

For thirty-five years I was blind to who Jesus is. I was a good girl with good morals, trying to get along in a world of unbelieving friends. Only one person had ever attempted to tell me about a relationship with Jesus when I was about thirty-four. When I finally saw John 3:3, "You must be born again to enter the kingdom of heaven," I was mad. I could have had a wonderful Christian life if only I had known. But no one told me.

What stops people from sharing such a wonderful gift? I believe our biggest enemy is fear. Fear of sounding foolish is pride. Fear of failure is not trusting God. Fear of rejection is not loving the other enough to lay down our lives. Fear is a deadly enemy that claims more souls than any other vice. Yet fear can be overcome. A sign posted during World War II read: "If your knees knock, kneel on them."

First of all, to share our faith, it is imperative that we receive the Holy Spirit. Jesus said in John 3:3, "You must be born again to see the kingdom of God." When you admit your sins to God, ask His forgiveness, acknowledge that Jesus died on the cross for those sins, and then ask Jesus into your heart as Lord and Savior, you have been born again. Jesus told His disciples, who were hiding in the upper room fearing they would be crucified just as Jesus was, "Peace be with you! As the Father has sent me, I am sending you," and then He said, "Receive the Holy Spirit" (John 20:22). The Holy Spirit removes the fear we have and gives us the power and gifts to do the work of God.

Before Jesus ascended into heaven, He commands them, "Do not leave Jerusalem, but wait for the gift my Father promised, which you have heard me speak about. For John baptized with water, but in a few days you will be baptized with the Holy Spirit" (Acts 1:4–5).

Verse 8 says, "But you will receive power when the Holy Spirit comes on you; and you will be my witnesses in Jerusalem, and in all Judea and Samaria, and to the ends of the earth." In chapter 2 the Holy Spirit comes upon them, and immediately they come out of hiding and start preaching the good news. Three thousand people became believers that day.

To receive the baptism of the Holy Spirit, ask Jesus for it. Just say, "Jesus, I ask for the baptism of the Holy Spirit and all the power and gifts that I will need to do Your will here on earth." God does not make things hard for us. He wants us to succeed.

The last thing our Good Shepherd did before He died on the cross was usher in a new believer hanging on the cross next to His. He not only used His life as an example, He used His mouth and talked to the thief. What if He had only prayed for him? What if He had not talked to him? What if in my dream I had only rowed away in my boat and never reached out to anyone?

Second, realize that "Love casts out fear" (1 John 4:18). Pray that God gives you a love for the lost. Ask Him to let you see them with His eyes. You will see many who wander aimlessly. They have no shepherd, no answers, nothing to hold on to. You will see hurting people everywhere.

Protesting is merely pointing a finger at others. Remember Jesus' words: "Forgive them, for they know not what they do." We seem to quickly forget what it was like to be blind. We also seem to forget that sheep follow a gentle voice, a voice that loves them, one they can trust.

Third, confess your fear as sin. Ask for forgiveness, and use your self-control to overcome it. God cannot find a lost lamb hidden by the darkness of sin, but when we cry out to Him, He hears us and comes to our rescue. He wants nothing more than your salvation and the salvation of everyone He sends your way.

Fourth, keep your armor on (see Eph. 6). Don't give Satan a foothold. I never realized that I took off the belt of truth each time I exaggerated, until one day I got a little carried away with a story about a miracle God used me in. "Wasn't My miracle good enough for you?" He asked me.

Fifth, use Revelation 12:11: "They overcame him [Satan] by the blood of the lamb, and the word of their testimony." No one can argue with your testimony. It is true and it is yours. Then tell them about the blood that was shed for them. God's love and grace abide in our victories. If you don't have a testimony to share, start obeying God's instructions. Lay hands on the sick. Pray with people. God will not let you down.

Sixth, realize that fear is overcome by confidence. Confidence comes by being sure of yourself and by trusting God. Being sure of yourself comes from practice. Practice brings success, which will bring a hunger for more. A quotation I once read said, "Do the thing you fear, and the death of fear is certain" (Grit). God calls us to have an abundant life. To live, love, and bless. The rewards are here for you now. Store up some treasures, some memories, some stories of victories to share with more of God's lost lambs.

CHAPTER 27

FAITHFUL IN LITTLE

WE HAD BEEN FAITHFUL in little. Starting with two sheep, we had now grown to one of the largest purebred Hampshire breeders in the state of Washington. Our sheep were strong, healthy, and cherished. But there were other sheep God was concerned with—sheep with two legs.

I was forty years old when I decided to go to college and learn bookkeeping on a computer. English 101 was a required class. Being much better with numbers than with spelling, I was a little hesitant about what kind of grade I would get. I discovered my teacher to be of the Mormon faith. So through several required essays, I chose to witness to her about "my Jesus." In the final essay, I explained how to receive Jesus as Lord and Savior.

She took the stack of papers home with her from all the students in her class. Her plan was to start correcting them the following day. That night, however, she had terrible chest pains. Thinking she was about to die, she wrote out her will as she awaited the paramedics. The next day the doctors told her it was stress and not her heart. As she lay in her hospital bed recuperating, she read my manuscript. I got an A and a note at the bottom. "Thank you, Barbara, for sharing this with me." God's timing is perfect.

I was inspired to take another communications class, so I signed up for public speaking next. Our first assignment was a two-minute speech telling why we were taking the class. I nervously explained that I had been born again and wanted to share the experience with other people in a more professional way. I wanted to be an evangelist.

We were given several assignments to speak. The first was on our favorite book and why. I spoke on the Bible. The second assignment was to tell of the most exciting day of our lives. I shared on being born again. The third was to speak on an emotion. I spoke on unconditional love. The class as a whole was to critique each speaker. Comments such as, "I didn't understand your topic," or, "You spoke too fast or you used too many *ands* and *uhs*," were typical. But the comments my classmates made on my papers were extremely encouraging. They wrote things like, "I didn't know God was real," "Could I speak to you after class?" and my favorite, "You are better than Billy Graham." Over half the class wound up giving their lives to Jesus by the end of the semester.

I forgot about bookkeeping and went on to interpersonal communications. Here I decided to keep my Christianity a secret for a while and make as many friends as I could first. Well, that lasted all of ten minutes. As we sat in a big circle the man next to me was to start. We were to tell what we expected to get out of taking the class. He started out by telling us that he was thirty-three years old and had terminal cancer. He could not do his labor job any longer, so he needed to be educated in another field, so he could support his wife and little girl as long as possible. Tears came to his eyes as he told us of his fight with depression at not getting to see his little girl grow up.

I couldn't stand it. "I died once," I spoke out, putting my hand tenderly on his, "and that is not the end. It's just like closing your eyes for a moment and opening them again. You are still the same person, only the pain is gone. If you ask Jesus into your heart, and your family does the same, one day you will all be together again in heaven."

There went my cover, but an interesting thing happened as a result. A journalism major in the class approached me later that day and asked if she could do an interview about my death experience for a college newspaper article she wanted to write. A few days later she had a photographer take my picture and then led me to a classroom that was not being used so we could have some privacy.

"Do you mind if I record our interview?" she asked as she turned on a machine sitting on the desk.

"Now, I'm going to be Barbara Walters, and you be my interviewee. It will be fun. Start by telling me about your death experience."

"Well," I began, "I was twenty-one at the time and pregnant with twins. I had complications and hemorrhaged to death in the hospital intensive care unit. I remember having a lot of pain in my right arm, where they had been putting in blood that had been refrigerated.

"I looked up, then closed my eyes and opened them again to see my body above me. I was falling down, down, down, looking up at the back of my body. I know now I was on my way to hell."

"How did you know that?" She leaned forward, her long blond hair falling over her shoulder.

"I didn't know right then, but since I have been born again, I understand it."

"Tell me about being born again."

Tears began to fall from her pretty blue eyes as I began to share my experiences with her. I told her about a time my daughter had been dating a darling sixteen-year-old boy. He was, however, into heavy metal music—AC/DC—and Dungeons and Dragons. We thought we could somehow reach him and took him to church with us one Sunday.

The pastor that day chose to speak on being unequally yoked. He said that we were not even to date an unbeliever, because it was like putting a ball and chain around our foot. We would have to drag them along every time we wanted to go to church or a Bible study. One day we would weary and quit coming. Then he turned to the teens and said, "Don't play with dead kids." The message hit us right between the eyes, although it went right over her boyfriend's head.

I hadn't known why I was telling her this part of my experiences with the Lord, but the Holy Spirit did. My young interviewer had been rejected by her boyfriend's Christian parents. He had tried to explain to her, but she had never understood until then. Tears spilled and sobs remain on the tape we recorded that day as she gave her life to Jesus.

When the college newspaper came out, there I was on the front page. The Lord saw to it that every student there had a chance to know Him because I had been faithful in taking the first step. He once said to me, "You have not walked until you take the first step." Take one, and just see what happens.

To order additional copies of

Heart of a Shepherd

send $12.95 U.S. plus $4.95 shipping and handling to

Books, Etc.
PO Box 1406
Mukilteo, WA 98275

or have your credit card ready and call

(800) 917-BOOK